101 Ways
to Get
and Keep
His Attention

MICHELLE
McKINNEY
HAMMOND

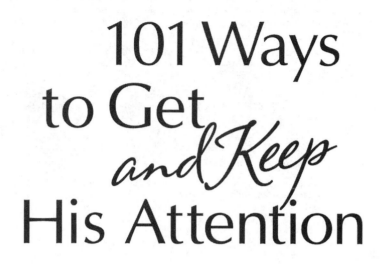

101 Ways
to Get *and Keep*
His Attention

MICHELLE
McKINNEY
HAMMOND

HARVEST HOUSE™PUBLISHERS

EUGENE, OREGON

Cover by Koechel Peterson & Associates, Inc., Minneapolis, Minnesota

Cover image © Meiklejohn, UK Gianelli/Images.com, Inc.

Published in association with the literary agency of Alive Communications, Inc., 7680 Goddard Street, Suite 200, Colorado Springs, CO 80920

101 WAYS TO GET AND KEEP HIS ATTENTION
Copyright © 2003 by Michelle McKinney Hammond
Published by Harvest House Publishers
Eugene, Oregon 97402

Library of Congress Cataloging-in-Publication Data
    McKinney Hammond, Michelle, 1957-
        101 ways to get and keep his attention / Michelle McKinney Hammond.
            p. cm.
        ISBN 0-7369-1136-7
        1. Single women—Religious life. 2. Single women—Conduct of life. 3. Man-woman relationships—Biblical teaching. 4. Man-woman relationships—Religious aspects—Christianity. I. Title: One hundred and one ways to get and keep his attention.
        II. Title: One hundred one ways to get and keep his attention. III. Title.
        BV4596.S5M34 2003
        248.8'43--dc21   2003001985

Printed in the United States of America.

04 05 06 07 08 09 10 11 / BP-KB / 10

*This book is dedicated to all the women who
long for love—
to give as well as receive.
Remember, perfect love casts out all fear
and opens the door for endless possibilities...*

Acknowledgments

To my Harvest House family—thank you for not only nurturing my creativity, but challenging me to grow.

Shana—thanks for reining me in, 'cause you know I like to keep it real, girl!

Betty, Barb, LaRae, Carolyn, Julie, Teresa, Brynn, Jill, Annie—you all are the best. I truly appreciate and love you.

Bob Jr.—the body reflects the head. God bless you for your leadership, caring, attention, and integrity.

Chip—thanks for always being there.

All my loved ones—you know who you are. Thank you for sacrificing time with me so that I can share with others. Your presence and support keep me going.

To all the men who dared to be honest so that I could write this book—I thank you. Words cannot express how valuable and life-changing your input was to me.

Contents

The Thing About Men...

en! What is it about them? What do they want anyway? Whether single or married, can anyone figure them out? What are they looking for in a woman? Do they even *know?* Of course they do! Do we take the time to ask them becomes the bigger question.

Well, I decided to ask men of all sizes, shapes, colors, ages, and walks of life what gets their attention. But more importantly, what *keeps* their attention. The results were rather surprising. Their answers didn't vary that much. The greatest discovery from my survey is: We women overthink this thing called attraction. We magnify the miniscule and overlook things that are major deal makers or breakers in their minds.

I polled men from college age to late seventies. Believers and nonbelievers. Professionals, blue collar, entrepreneurs, and unemployed. Men of different races and backgrounds. Their needs and wants, though greatly detailed, were pretty basic. The biggest shocker came from Christian men—the characteristics they look for in a woman were not that different from those who did not claim to be "religious." This led me to a great revelation. While women who know Christ are striving to live a life that is pleasing to God, they cannot ignore the fact that they are dealing with a man who is first human, then spiritual.

7

The big dilemma for the average Christian male is that he knows what he *should* desire in a woman as a new creature in Christ. But there are also the things he *really* desires—natural desires that do not go away when he becomes a Christian. Because no one discusses these issues or gives men permission to feel what they feel, many experience anxiety—locked in a secret battle with themselves. To admit they want a beautiful woman seems "carnal." However, the Bible never plays down the beauty of women or men. In fact, it is celebrated and sung about in Scripture. How do we find a balance for these God-given desires that have been perverted by the ways of the world?

Men are not the only ones facing a dilemma. Most women who come to know Christ are anxious to cast off their worldly ways, but they find themselves at a loss as to how to balance their spiritual walk with the art of natural attraction. Fear causes them to go to the other extreme—forsaking natural God-given gifts that were meant to nurture fruitful relationships. In the end, after many disappointments, they wonder why true love, commitment, and romance seem so elusive.

Well, you can count on me to give you the inside scoop. Rather than give away names and internal secrets, I will simply deal with the information that was so freely shared with me. Then, of course, it's always a good idea to ask the One who created men. And, might I add, created them to reflect His own heart. Who could comprehend their hearts better than the One who shaped them and intimately knows them? It is always wise to examine the natural as well as the spiritual when dealing with something as powerful as love.

This has become more apparent to me as I travel the country talking with men and women who are struggling with their relationships. Women wonder why men in the church are venturing beyond church walls to find mates. Don't they want a godly mate? The answer is yes, but they don't want a boring one. They want a woman who is sold out to the Lord but still in possession of all the attributes they expect to find in a woman. Godly does not mean up-tight and puritanical. We simply must learn how to love and be loved in the right context.

You might ask why am I writing this book. The answer is simple. Relationships in the church are in trouble. Satan, who hates marriage, is busy keeping good, single men and women apart or attacking marriage by keeping hus-bands and wives at odds with one another. Recently, I spoke at a church. Afterward, one husband came to my book table asking for everything I had to give to his wife. I complimented his wife on the outfit she was wearing and got an earful from this man. He informed me he had bought her the suit and she had never even thanked him for it. It didn't stop there. He went on to tell me that he did the cooking, cleaning, and laundry at his house and his wife did nothing. He felt unloved and could I please talk to his wife! I was taken aback. Here was a woman who knew how to praise the Lord but not how to please her husband! In her mind, she felt she was a godly woman.

We must all be careful of being so heavenly minded we are no earthly good. The Bible clearly states that if we say we love the Lord but don't love our brother, we are a liar! Love is only evidenced by our actions. Of course, I did not have all the facts about their relationship and, therefore, would not judge this lovely woman or speak against her. Perhaps he had wounded her, and she was bound in un-forgiveness. As women of God, we must be able to bring our wounds to Christ, and speak the truth in love to those we are in a relationship with.

Later, I received a letter from yet another sister in the Lord who admitted to not paying attention to her husband after having a baby. Now he was seeking attention from someone else. How could she get his attention back, she asked. She was at a loss as to what to do. This man was also a believer in the church! It is alarming to read statistics that report marriages in the church are failing at the same rate as marriages in the secular arena. Time is not being taken to counsel women and men on how to find and maintain fulfilling and joyous relationships. This area, so overlooked, is important because victorious singles and happy marriages are a great witness to the world. They translate the love and power of God into a practical application that can be grasped and imitated.

A happier story is one of a wife who, after hearing me speak, went home and put my suggestions into action. The next day, a glowing husband and wife stood before me. The husband thanked me for my influence in his wife's life. This wife emailed me months later to tell me of the profound effect her changed behavior had on their marriage. She was still on cloud nine!

There are countless examples I could give on the difference that attention to a few details can make in your interaction with men, whether single or married. I will be sharing about both types of relationships in this book. At times, I will clarify what is appropriate for singles versus married women.

A word of caution here: Some of you might find yourself being challenged on different personal habits and attitudes. I must admit that I, too, was confronted about some areas where I could tighten up my act as I began to record the revelations I was given. Some of you will have to deal with unresolved issues and personal fears that have been hindering you from having fulfilling relationships with members of the opposite sex. You may have chosen to avoid these issues in the past; however, if you want to eventually get married or have a joyful marriage, you will have to deal with the reality of where you presently live and incorporate the changes you need to make in order to move forward and achieve your personal goals. Though this will require great soul-searching and dealing with your personal inventory, I pray you will adopt the same attitude I did. Embrace the information and put it to good use. At times, I will share principles and explain them to the best of my ability. Other times, I will simply share a small phrase that can make a big difference in your interaction with members of the opposite sex. Although you may be convicted as you realize there are parts of yourself that you have not nurtured, don't fall into condemnation. Celebrate the opportunity to become an even better woman than you already are. As you begin to renew your mind, get ready for the transformation that will allow you to reap new results in your life.

Keep in mind this is not a contest. This is about acquiring wisdom to become: first, the woman God wants you to be, and second, a woman the right man will desire. Be the best you can be and leave the rest to God's divine purpose and timing for your life. This is the key to not only being irresistible, but for living a life full of joy as you revel in being a complete woman from the inside out. The type of woman men not only notice, but love to be around. Keep in mind, the same thing it took to get him will be the same thing it takes to keep him, so never relax your womanly wiles.

On that note, I won't keep you in suspense any longer.

So you really want to know how to get the attention of that special someone? Do you need to know how to keep the attention of the one you love? Pull up a chair, girl, and let's start at the beginning.

The Physical

Sight

The Body

The Eye of the Beholder

We all know that men are visual creatures, but we shouldn't stop there. We must examine the whole man. Men are three-dimensional beings. They are living souls who have a spirit that resides in a body. This means that we must appeal to all three levels of their makeup—physical, emotional, and spiritual. Beyond this, they have five senses that involve how they respond—to sight, sound, smell, taste, and touch. When getting a man's attention, you can appeal to one level and affect one sense. However, to keep that man's interest, you must involve all levels of his being as well as all of his senses.

Where do we begin? In the obvious place. In order to capture his heart, you've got to catch his eye first. So let's begin with the eye-gate. What first catches his eye? The physical realm...hmmm, it's not as bad as you think. You will be surprised to find that while we are examining ourselves under a high-powered microscope for all of our various real and imagined flaws, men view women quite differently. Every man has his favorite feature. Lips, legs, eyes, oh my! It is a varied list depending on who is looking your way. So we will take a look at them all. Something about you might catch his eye that is seemingly insignificant, even quirky, in fact. Aaah, but to hold his gaze, the picture of you must be completed, but not exactly the way you think...

Eyes

You have stolen my heart, my sister, my bride;
you have stolen my heart with one glance of
your eyes... (Song of Songs 4:9).

*H*ow many songs have been sung about what a woman's eyes do to a man? We've heard that the eyes are the windows to the soul so often it has become trite, but it is true. What is it about the eyes? Though silent, they speak volumes. They tell a man if we are angry, sad, happy, approachable, or un-approachable.

In the beginning, God made all fruit pleasing to the eye, including us. We are the fruit of His omniscient womb. He fashioned us not just as a reflection of Himself, but as something that would be nice to look at. He formed women to attract men. This is not a bad or sinful thing. However, how we use what God has given us can either work for or against us. What do your eyes say?

Let's consider the effect a woman's eyes can have. They have the power to arrest a man, to captivate, invite, or deter his approach.

Hmmm, the lover in Song of Songs told the beloved that her eyes were like the pools of Heshbon. The word *Heshbon* means "stronghold." A stronghold is a place of no escape. Now that's deep. He asked her later in chapter 6, verse 5 to turn her eyes away from him because they overwhelmed him...oooh, this is juicy stuff! The girl hadn't said a word, yet she had captured this man with her eyes.

Her eyes were also like doves. Soft and gentle, not arro-gant and bold. They were eyes that beckoned one to come closer. What do yours say? Are they filled with the pain of past relationships? Hardened by mistrust? Before you can beckon love and find favor in the eyes of another, your eyes must be refocused on the joy set before you.

Submit your fears and disappointments to the Lord and dwell on His promises so that He can fill your eyes with the light of His love. A light that will attract the right man to follow the path to your heart.

> *Your eye is the lamp of your body. When your eyes are good, your whole body also is full of light. But when they are bad, your body also is full of darkness* (Luke 11:34).

Lips

> *Your lips are like a scarlet ribbon; your mouth is lovely* (Song of Songs 4:3).

Lips come in all sizes and shapes—full, thin, voluptuous, pouty, streamlined—you name it. And now with the help of cosmetic surgery, we can make them look any way we want. One thing cosmetic surgery cannot do, though, is make those lips, no matter what size, appealing to a man if they are subconsciously taut and rigid from churning emotions within.

Funny how we can tell if someone is upset by either looking into their eyes or observing the set of their lips. If someone's lips are stiff or turned downward, we know that person is not a happy camper. They are upset about something. We temper our words, fearing a sharp answer. However, lips that are soft and relaxed let us know the coast is clear.

How many millions of dollars do women spend on lipstick, yet no fabulous color can conceal the way they feel? The lips reveal a lot!

Are your lips soft, inviting pleasant conversation, or do they threaten a rebuke? Do they bid welcome, or are they stiff with pride or suspicion? Perhaps it's time to spit out whatever tastes bitter within and fill yourself with goodness. Yes, that's it! Though men may fail you and life might disappoint, taste and see that God is good. His promises are enough to fill you with hope and make you look like the cat that swallowed the canary. Go ahead, lick your lips—allow them to be one of your most outstanding features.

> *Your lips have been anointed with grace, since God has blessed you forever* (Psalm 45:2).

A Welcoming Smile

*P*erhaps things are causing you to conceal those pearly whites. Maybe grim lips are hiding the beautiful inner you. Deal with the inside and set the outside free. A smile can do more than words in many instances. When asked what made a woman approachable, more men than not said a simple smile was enough to suffice. All they needed was a signal that the coast was clear to approach. An expressionless look did not make them feel safe. Even if the rest of the package looked nice, they were sure to pass on the contents.

All dressed up, looking good, and still wondering why the world is passing you by? Better get happy and smile, girl!

Beautiful Teeth

Your teeth are like a flock of sheep coming up from the washing. Each has its twin, not one of them is alone (Song of Songs 6:6).

Virtually every single toothpaste on the market has added a new ingredient: whitener. It is as if a news flash hit all the makers of toothpaste at the same time. Gleaming white teeth are desirable; healthy is no longer enough.

I must admit, after enduring braces in high school (and not the cool clear ones that they have now either!), teeth are a biggie for me as well. Bad teeth can be a deal breaker. But strong, clean, even white teeth say that person cares about their diet as well as their hygiene. This rates high on the desirability scale for men. It was amazing how many of them brought this one up.

So, even if you have fabulous teeth but no one sees them, what does it profit you? Take a moment to see what your mouth says about you.

Complexion

Do not stare at me because I am dark, because I am darkened by the sun. My mother's sons were angry with me and made me take care of the vineyards; my own vineyard I have neglected (Song of Songs 1:6).

Fair, dark, ruddy, pale as the moon, dark as the night, café au lait, caramel...we come in many shades and flavors that are appealing to various men. Do not despise what someone else may celebrate.

Beautiful Skin

Who is this that appears like the dawn, fair as the moon, bright as the sun, majestic as the stars in procession? (Song of Songs 6:10).

Isn't it interesting that the Shulammite woman in Song of Songs saw herself one way and her lover saw her in an entirely different light? He saw her as fair while she considered the color of her skin undesirable. Fair in this context actually means beautiful. What he saw was not the color but the condition of her skin. It was lustrous and satiny smooth. It had been kissed by the sun and was radiant with a healthy glow. Her skin was rich with vitality—it was alive. It was skin he wanted to touch, though he reserved that impulse for a more appropriate time.

It doesn't matter what shade or flavor you are. Care for your skin tenderly and allow its finer properties to shine through. You never know who is looking at you...

Hair

Your hair is like a flock of goats descending from Gilead (Song of Songs 6:5).

*O*kay, ladies, let's get real about the hair. This one is a biggie. Men love hair that moves and has a quiet luster that catches the light—fluid, rich, and full. Now we all have different textures, lengths, and colors of hair. What is important here is healthy hair that is not forced in its presentation. Au naturel is the vote from the menfolk. They want to enjoy what they see and anticipate permission to touch it at the right time.

Are men opposed to our fascination with weaves and extensions? Only if they look too done, so pay attention to the fine details if this is the route you want to take. Truly our hair is our glory, but wear it well, my sister.

Your head crowns you like Mount Carmel. Your hair is like royal tapestry; the king is held captive by its tresses (Song of Songs 7:5).

Hands

*T*his is purely subjective but survey says—men are afraid of nails that look like weapons. Strong, sensitive hands are appealing in their book. Clean, neat, cultured nails will do. They don't even care about polish (well, they do if it's looking as though it's time for a manicure). This speaks of the time and attention you pay to yourself in their eyes.

Take the time to cultivate even the little things. The little things become major in their eyes. When you extend your hand, make sure it is a hand they want to hold. Have hands they long to have touch them tenderly, in a reassuring pat only a wife can offer her man...Hands that are the finishing touch of graceful, welcoming arms.

Arms

*Y*es, arms are important. It's funny what men notice. Strong arms speak of strength and fitness. They don't need to be buff; toned will suffice. It's amazing how quickly sometimes minor things become major. In the mind of a husband or a man considering a woman as a potential mate, hands are made for touching and loving them. Arms are for embracing and being capable of handling the tasks at hand.

If you're married, go ahead and reach out to your man. This is part of a man's love language and has tremendous impact.

Singles, be careful! Don't start fires you can't put out. The book of Ecclesiastes says there is a time to embrace and a time to refrain from embracing. God places a high price on a man being intimate with you—one of a lifetime commitment. Maintain His standard and conduct yourself accordingly.

Neck

Your cheeks are beautiful with earrings, your neck with strings of jewels (Song of Songs 1:10).

It's no small wonder that a woman can take any part of her body and make it speak. We all laugh at the sister-girl neck roll. And yet it says a lot. It says, "How dare you! Don't you *ever* do that again! Stop right there, mister. Don't even think about getting any closer!" A neck can reflect defiance or submission, pride or humility. A neck can say, "Get back!" or "I'm open to listen." Mmhm, a neck can say all of that and have the capacity to portray a vulnerability a man finds so appealing. It can be a tender place. Its tenderness is particularly attractive to men.

Even God talks about stiff-necked women being a turn off. We adorn our necks, we perfume them, but do we understand the power of them? The grace and elegance they can portray? The soft, alluring beauty they possess? The stubbornness they can reveal, even when we try to put our best face forward? Perhaps we would walk more carefully if we really understood their mystique.

Your neck is like the tower of David, built with elegance (Song of Songs 4:4).

11 Legs

How beautiful your sandaled feet, O prince's daughter! Your graceful legs are like jewels, the work of a craftsman's hands (Song of Songs 7:1).

*L*ong legs, short legs, skinny ones, thick ones—it's every man for himself in this category. To shave or not to shave—even this cannot be pinned down, although I dare say the general populace leans toward the Nair-smooth model as politically correct and desirable. To this I say: Find the right dress or skirt length to complement what you've got and then strut your stuff with graceful confidence.

12 Feet

*W*e know many a leg man, *but feet, Michelle*?! Yeah, girl, feet. Survey says men are checking out our feet. Are they clean and neatly manicured, or are they hard, calloused, and looking worse for wear? Your feet are an indication of how much attention you pay to your personal grooming. Do you take the time to deal with things that are not so obvious?

Do you love yourself enough to pay attention to all the details of your appearance? How we take care of ourselves says a lot to a man—it lets him know how you view yourself. Just remember, if you don't take good care of yourself, who will? How precious is your body to you? Take care of it—from the top of your head to the tips of your toes. All your features deserve honor as part of one great body.

A Great Body

Your navel is a rounded goblet that never lacks blended wine. Your waist is a mound of wheat encircled by lilies. Your two breasts are like two fawns, twins of a gazelle (Song of Songs 7:2-3).

Okay, okay, so men like breasts, hips, breasts, legs, breasts...perhaps it's the mother thing. This is another area where the style, size, and shape preference is purely subjective. So here's what I say. Accentuate the positive and downplay the negative. Dress according to your shape. The right foundation is definitely something to consider here. Victoria's secret is that she makes a foundation for everyone to enhance what nature gave them. Start from the top down with the right underwear. The right outfit can look all wrong if the foundation isn't together. If you are small, you still need to have the right bra to ensure a beautiful profile. For those who are bountifully endowed, use bras with cotton straps to keep yourself firmly in place and present a flawless finish. Whatever your size, consult with someone who specializes in selecting the right pieces to present your best figure.

Bodyshapers pull up what needs to be up and suck in needless extras. Set the stage for the dress you want to wear and then enter looking your best. Whether a size 2 or a size 20, neatness goes a long way when it comes to being in great form.

Posture

Your stature is like that of the palm (Song of Songs 7:7-8).

Ooowee! I mean King Solomon had a rap, didn't he? But let's face it, he was only saying what every man thinks but doesn't have the nerve to utter. The way we stand, the way we carry our bodies speaks volumes. There is something about a woman who walks upright with her head held high. There is peace with herself in every step. She likes herself. She feels good about herself.

Now close your eyes and imagine that same woman slumped over, shoulders curved forward, neck bent, head hung over. Is that a desirable picture to you? Not only does it say this person is feeling sorry for herself, it's not a healthy stance at all. Body language—that's what we're talking about here—plain and simple. How you carry your-self makes you approachable or wards off all interested parties. Take a moment to check out how you stand.

Dreess

On the third day Esther put on her royal robes and stood in the inner court of the palace, in front of the king's hall. The king was sitting on his royal throne in the hall, facing the entrance. When he saw Queen Esther standing in the court, he was pleased with her and held out to her the gold scepter that was in his hand (Esther 5:1-2).

That must have been some dress Esther had on! What kind of dress would make a man want to give all of his power to a woman? Contrary to popular belief, flesh is not the attracting factor, mystery is. Some men have double standards about the way a woman dresses. Yes, he will turn and gawk at a woman walking down the street who is showing more than she should, but does he want the woman on his arm to dress in the same manner? Absolutely not! He may be attracted to the scantily dressed woman but not respect her or take her seriously at all.

I always ask the question: *Would you be proud to meet Jesus in what you are wearing?* That settles it, dress accordingly. Now that doesn't mean your stuff has to be up to the top of your neck or hitting the floor. Simply dress with taste and modesty. Leave something to the imagination. Leave that man wanting to know more about you. Give him hints but not the full conclusion. Dress carefully and effectively. Soft, feminine, and inviting, but without displaying things that only your mate should see. Let your dress speak volumes about your character—modest not brazen, godly not worldly. Highlight your best qualities without distracting from your overall natural beauty. The rule for dressing is less can be more, and I am not speaking of fabric. Dress the way you want to be perceived. If you are a queen, dress like one.

*I also want women to dress modestly, with de-
cency and propriety* (1 Timothy 2:9).

16 Movement

*While he was still talking with them, Rachel
came with her father's sheep, for she was a
shepherdess. When Jacob saw Rachel daughter
of Laban, his mother's brother, and Laban's sheep,
he went over and rolled the stone away from the
mouth of the well and watered his uncle's sheep.
Then Jacob kissed Rachel and began to weep
aloud* (Genesis 29:9-11).

I wonder if Rachel had a special sway when she walked
that could have interrupted a man's conversation. Remember the girl from Ipanema? An entire song was sung in trib-
ute to her walk and the way it affected those who saw
her...my, my, my. I wonder if she went to finishing school.

Whatever happened to finishing schools? Where you
learned to walk, sit, and hold your hands a certain way?
Where you learned to be a lady? Now it's every woman for
herself! And today's shoes aren't doing anybody any favors.
Small wonder some women are mincing around while
others are clumping as if trying to crush grapes in wine season. Amazing. Men design those fabulous mules and then
expect us to walk gracefully. There is a way to walk and
then there is a *way* to walk.

Men observe how women walk and draw conclusions
based on what they see. I once overheard a man who was
watching a woman cross the street say, "She walks as if she

is enjoying herself." Sure enough, I followed the direction of his eyes, and there was this woman taking her time, her hips swaying gently as if she was walking to music none of us could hear. She was like a poem, moving in slow motion through the rest of the crowd as they made their way from point A to B. It brought to mind the song, "She walks in beauty..."

What does your walk say? That you are on a mission? Or that all is well with your soul and you are enjoying the day? Better walk lightly, someone might be watching.

And it's not just your walk; it's all your movements—the way you do the things you do. How you bend over to pick something up, the little way you flick your hair over your shoulder or innocently stretch without thinking. Men take note of all these things.

Perhaps a turn of the head or a movement of the arm reminds them of something pleasant buried in their spirit. It connects and surfaces longings they believe we can answer. Is this something you can totally control? Probably not. But just remember that your inner workings will be manifested in your body language. So make sure all is well with your soul and reflect it in all you do.

Enjoying Life

Everyone loves to see a parade. To go to a party. To share a joke. To enjoy life. Everyone wants to be a part of a celebration. The greatest way to attract interest is to possess what someone else wants. Ladies, if you don't enjoy your life, why would anyone want to be a part of it? This is crucial.

Begin today to live life as if it were the gala of the century. Enjoy yourself. From the simple pleasures to more complicated delights, select one and enjoy living in the moment. Embrace opportunities and experiences that put a spark in your eye and a bounce in your step. Joy is irresistible. Everyone is always seeking more, and if you have a surplus to pour out, believe me, someone will come for a drink. Joy speaks of more than the ability to amuse yourself. It speaks of wholeness, confidence, a settled heart that is comfortable.

Choose to be joyful when you wake. Make cheerfulness a habit in your life. It's entirely up to you. Apply it to your heart the way you would makeup to your face. Joy acts like a magnet, drawing others to itself. In a man's eyes, joy speaks of more than just momentary enjoyment. Joy is pregnant with promise. Promises of pleasures that have yet to be revealed. Promises he will be determined to discover. For singles, it is the mystery of the promise that inspires a man to commit. Therefore, keep your secrets until you have the blessing of God to reveal them. Married ladies, don't keep your husband guessing too long. Allow him to discover the source of your joy and share it with you in a delightful conspiracy. Always have new joys for him to discover—one surprise at a time.

Originality

So the LORD God caused a deep sleep to fall upon the man, and he slept; then He took one of his ribs, and closed up the flesh at that place. And the LORD God fashioned into a woman the rib

*which He had taken from the man, and brought
her to the man. And the man said, "This is now
bone of my bones, And flesh of my flesh; She
shall be called Woman, Because she was taken
out of Man"* (Genesis 2:21-23 NASB).

Remember, there is only one of you. You were carefully
fashioned by God to complement the man He knew He
would place you beside. Many ask me if there is only one
man for every woman. My reply is always the same, "There
are many men you could settle for, but there is one that
God knows is best for you." When He decided to give
Adam a mate, he did not place Eve, Mary, and Sue before
him and allow him to pick. He designed one especially capable of meeting all of Adam's needs. So embrace your
originality—the things about you that set you apart from
every other woman on the face of the earth.

Just as there was only one Eve, there is only one you
who does things the way you do. Now these are a little
more nebulous, harder to pinpoint because they are so personal. Defining these things releases you to be yourself.
There are the unexplained things that every man likes
about a woman, from the way she wrinkles her nose to the
way she orders her food and insists on putting the bread to
the side of her sandwich. Several movies come to mind
where the heroine had "quirky" down to a science, yet the
man in pursuit of her loved every minute of it. Why? Because her quirks made her unique. There was no one else
quite like her, and every other woman seemed boring in
comparison. The men in these cute romantic movies loved
watching the women who had won their hearts because
they were just so...well...different, intriguing, cute! One
man told me, when listing the peculiarities of the woman
he was in love with, that he didn't love her in spite of her
idiosyncrasies, he loved her *because* of them.

Who can say why we develop the habits we do? They are a part of what makes us extraordinary women. If you were like everyone else, you would be common fare with no special value at all. But to have the added attraction of "nobody does it like you do" is the thing that sets you apart from the masses. This takes the pressure off of those who strive to be cookie-cutter models of someone they've seen and admire. There was only one Marilyn Monroe, one Dorothy Dandridge, one Audrey Hepburn—the rest have been poor imitations. Everyone can spot a reproduction of the real thing. It is never appreciated. There is only one you, and this is a good thing. Leave the imitations to someone else. Keep it real, 'cause believe me, the man for you will be able to tell the difference.

Willingness to Grow

Iron sharpens iron, so one man sharpens another (Proverbs 27:17).

Remember when people got married earlier? A young man and woman finished school, got married, had a family, and grew old together. In today's society, many are waiting until they're older to get married; however, it is my opinion that this is both good and bad. On the good side, you have to take time to discover who you really are, what you want, and what you don't want out of life as well as a marriage partner. The bad side is that we become set in our ways and form a lot of unrealistic expectations of what that person should bring to the party. Never mind if we are not a complete package ourselves; we want our man to be perfect. To have worked out all of his defects, show up, and make us happy...Sorry, ladies, this only happens in fairy tales.

Many men will observe a woman to discern if she is willing to grow with him, and he should. The truth of the matter is, we are all unfinished products. It is the experiences in life and our interaction with others that cause us to grow and become better people. Accepting a man for who he is, seeing his vast potential, and allowing him to grow into it is a rare gift that delights a man when he finds it. Why? Because he doesn't expect to. He has grown used to women who judge him by where he is, and what he has acquired, and either accept or disqualify him based on what she finds.

The bottom line is that most women are not willing to struggle, grow, and develop with a man. They have forgotten that God fashioned the woman to finish and complete the man. With this in mind, we bring a lot to a man's life that was sorely lacking before we entered his world. As women we see all the missing pieces, but we wrongly expect them to be in place when we arrive.

How do we overcome this? By casting off the independent thinking, the cynicism, and the jaded outlook we've acquired and become open to the endless possibilities that two are able to accomplish. Together, a man and a woman build a future filled with all the things they desire. They build a home and a life they can share.

Stop looking for the prince with the loaded wallet to arrive and carry you away. Life is too heavy. It is too much for one horse to carry. So go ahead, invite him down from the saddle, take his hand, and ask him to walk with you to the place where you both can grow together. He will love you for it.

Two are better than one because they have a good return for their labor (Ecclesiastes 4:9).

Spirit

Let your gentleness be evident to all. The Lord is near (Philippians 4:5).

*I*t's true, your spirit is visible. It is interesting how many men, when commenting on why they like a certain woman, will say, "Because she has spirit!" Now that usually means she has spunk, pizzazz, or a bit of fire in her character. However, men who are more settled in their own spirits look on the inside. They look for a woman with a beautiful spirit. This inner ingredient has an obvious outward manifestation.

Though I've spent quite a bit of time literally picking you apart, body part by body part, it is important to know your spirit affects all of the outward features that make up the whole. No amount of makeup can cover up an ugly or broken spirit. You can have the richest tresses, the most kissable lips, the most interesting walk, a bam-bam body, and still miss out by having innards that are not whole.

This is where the real beauty treatment must begin. Approaching the throne of grace with outstretched arms, asking the Lord to wash you, heal you, and beautify you from the inside out. Small wonder Paul warned in 1 Peter 3:3-5, "Your beauty should not come from outward adornment, such as braided hair and the wearing of gold jewelry and fine clothes. Instead, it should be that of your inner self, the unfading beauty of a gentle and quiet spirit, which is of great worth in God's sight. For this is the way the holy women of the past who put their hope in God used to make themselves beautiful." God is not the only one who finds this trait attractive.

What he inwardly longs for...

To touch
to hold you
would make me feel
as if I had just awakened...
stretching myself
to my full stature.
I imagine coming to life
inside your arms
and knowing
that there is nowhere else
I'd rather be,
for your softness
will feel so good,
so good to me...
I will measure myself by you
and how you fit
within my grasp,
molding to me,
filling all my empty spaces...
flesh to flesh
bone to bone
heart to heart
breath to breath

spirit to spirit.

So in sync

I am inclined to agree

that this is no stretch of my imagination

that we could,

indeed,

most infinitely

be

one…

The Intellect

Sound

The Soul

The Wonder of Words

With persuasive words she led him astray; she seduced him with her smooth talk. All at once he followed her like an ox going to the slaughter, like a deer stepping into a noose till an arrow pierces his liver, like a bird darting into a snare, little knowing it will cost him his life (Proverbs 7:21-23).

My, my! The power of a woman's words. Words are creative in nature and very powerful. When God spoke, things happened. Earth came into being. We were created in God's image; therefore, our words have power too. The power of life and death. We can breathe life into a romance by the things we say or wipe out all possibilities with one fateful sentence—the wrong sentence.

This brings me to a point that must be clarified before we go any further with this train of thought. God was the originator of romance and a woman's power. Satan perverted both of these gifts by influencing women to use them in the wrong context. The woman described in the passage above was an adulterous woman, not a good woman. Whether married or single, sexual intimacy without the benefit of the marital commitment is more than a lie, it is a sin. Sin with deep and lasting consequences, regardless of God's graciousness to forgive. Adultery and fornication will always lead to death—not just for the man who has been seduced, but for the woman who chooses to initiate or partake in such behavior. Death to your spiritual and, in many cases, physical well-being. Death to inner peace, self-esteem, and self-respect.

Despite her intentions, how was this woman's approach effective? Perhaps if she had done with her husband all the things she did with this stranger on the street, her marriage would have been a happier one. We will never know. Obviously, she knew what to do to get the attention of a man. Married women should take note and single women should file this information until God blesses them to put it into practice. Let's take note of what she did. She dressed seductively and prepared herself for attracting love. She appealed to all of this man's senses. Sight—she made herself attractive. Sound—she gave him an invitation he couldn't refuse. Smell—she anointed herself with fragrant oils and promised him perfumed sheets and sweet-smelling surroundings. Taste—she prepared delectable foods, which I'm sure had the qualities of being aphrodisiacs. Touch—she embraced him and made him forget himself with her nearness. All things that every married woman has license to do with her husband. And if you have this license, you should take full advantage and recognize it as a privilege not given to all. Remember, most men, Christian or not, harbor fantasies. Fantasies that only a wife should make come true. There is plenty of room within godly confines to bring pleasure to the heart of your man and make his dreams a reality.

Compliments

Let my mouth be filled with thy praise and with thy honour all the day. (Psalm 71:8 KJV).

et's face it, praise is music to a man's ears. Why? Men are made in the image of God, and what does He crave from us? Worship, honor, and praise! Men are no different. They like to be noticed and appreciated. In this case, compliments will get you where you want to go. In the heart of every man is a little boy who likes to be built up: "Ooh, don't you look nice!" "Wow, you did that?!" "Hey, that's a really great idea. You are so smart." Just remember that as God does not like false praise, neither do men. Give praise from a pure heart.

I have a feeling some of you are rolling your eyes right now, but wait a minute. How do you feel when he tells you how nice you look? What is good for the goose is good for the gander. And trust me, if you don't do it, someone else will.

The story in 2 Samuel 6:16 says that when David returned home with the ark of the Lord, he danced in the streets until he danced out of his clothes. He then went home intending to bless his household. But upon returning home, he got no congratulations from his wife Michal. Instead, she berated him and basically told him he looked like an idiot dancing in front of a bunch of servant girls almost naked. To which he replied, he was pleased to humiliate himself before the Lord. But it didn't end there! He told her the servant girls of whom she spoke would still respect him. If he didn't get respect and praise from her, he knew where to get it. The sad story ends by David simply walking past her. He never blessed her, and she remained loveless and childless for the rest of her life.

Whether single or married, withholding praise from your man will cause unfruitfulness in the relationship. Unfruitfulness goes far beyond bearing children. There is the fruit of the Spirit that becomes even more lush through love. Goodness, kindness, patience…you know the list. You get what you give. A man needs and desires praise and honor from his woman. Consider your words and remember that one woman's trash will always be another woman's treasure. Don't leave your man as an open mark for another woman to discover. Let him find all he needs in you.

Interesting Conversation

$\mathcal{M}$usic videos have it all wrong. It's not walking around with everything showing, or even your ability to shake it up. The big question on the minds of men is: Can you captivate his mind with your conversation? This was high on the list, ladies. Every man I interviewed said they wanted a woman who had something to say. Stimulating conversation. Something that makes his mind work creatively! But be careful—that doesn't mean they like know-it-alls.

If your man likes sports and you aren't interested, you need to pay attention just enough to ask questions. Have an odd statistic or something interesting to say about his areas of interest—bring something new to the conversation. Try an attention-grabbing factoid to share that he might not know about. Sometimes married women lose ground with their husbands when their only conversation is about the

house or the kids. Single and married women must understand that men need mental stimulation. They are visionar-
ies, so we have to keep those word pictures coming.
Boredom equals wandering minds and eyes when it comes
to men.

Married men are not only looking for a wife and lover,
they are looking for a friend and a companion. Single men,
when considering a woman as a potential mate, want to
know they will like and enjoy as well as love her, because
she is a well-rounded person. So as Luci Swindoll would
say, "Don't just be interested, be interesting!"

Honesty

*The heart of her husband trusts in her, and he
will have no lack of gain. She does him good,
and not harm, all the days of her life* (Proverbs
31:11-12 RSV).

There is a reason honesty headed the list in my poll. Satan has done his homework well. He causes mistrust between the sexes by persuading women that men can't be
faithful and convincing men that women can't be trusted.
Every man on my poll said they had to have a woman they
could trust. Faithfulness and honesty were high priorities.
Trustworthiness is the first characteristic listed in the de-
scription of the virtuous woman in Proverbs 31.

What we have to understand is that men are afraid of
us. They know how powerful we are. They instinctively
concur that we can mess up their minds and render them

inoperable. In a world where the pressure for men to succeed is at an all time high, they can't afford to rest their hearts in the wrong place.

When you set the stage for honesty and transparency with a man, he will begin to relax and open the grasp he keeps on his heart. But the moment you give him any reason to doubt you, he will be off and running. Don't play games. Keep what is precious to yourself (past hurts or challenges) and release them to him one gem at a time when his love for you has been established and he can handle what you expose. Even in withholding information, remain honest. "I'm not really ready to share that yet." Whatever "that" might be, at least it lets him know that he has hit a soft spot in you. Together you can build a solid relationship foundation based on truth and honesty—a safe harbor for both your hearts.

Teamwork

Better to live in a desert than with a quarrelsome and ill-tempered wife (Proverbs 21:19).

*M*ost men are competitive but not argumentative. They don't like drama. As the Bible says, how can two walk together unless they agree? (See Amos 3:3.) This is so true. The world screams loudly enough. A woman should be an oasis for her man, not an additional source of tension or strife. Does that mean you should be a doormat? No. It merely means you must learn to accentuate the positive and minimize the negative. Find common ground. Don't be quick to challenge and disagree. Remember, you were made to be a man's partner. This calls for teamwork. Team members don't always agree, yet they work together to find solutions.

Allow him to lead. Yes, submit. Ooh! There's that word we don't like—submission. However, take a new look at that word and see it as your friend and not your enemy. Submission is merely being a cooperative member of the team. Being willing to work with the other player. *Submission puts you in the position to be blessed, covered, protected, and provided for.* It also enables a man to rise to the occasion and be the man he was created to be. So by all means, learn the art of give and take. Let him feel secure that you are for him and not against him.

Encouragement

Somebody had the right idea when they wrote the song, "Let's Hear It for the Boy!" Indeed, let's hear it. Everyone can use a word of encouragement to strengthen them and send them on their way. Now I'm hearing a bit of murmuring…"Well, what do I get out of this deal? Why do they need all the propping up?" You get a man doing his best to impress you and gain your admiration. That's what you get. When you let him know you believe in him, in his ability to accomplish his goals and dreams, he races for the finish line with you in mind.

Should he fail or fall, you will be the first person he seeks for comfort, to hear your words that will help him get back up and at 'em. To be viewed as a source of solace, as a safe harbor where he can store his dreams, is an incredible thing. It becomes the glue that bonds you together. And remember: you get what you give.

Reassurance

"I believe in you..."

"Everything will be all right..." (no matter what you're

thinking)

"You can count on me..."

"I understand how you feel..."

"We will make it through this."

Laughter

A merry heart doeth good like a medicine
(Proverbs 17:22 KJV).

Laughter is contagious. It dries tears and chases the blues
and cares of the day away. I find it interesting that so many
women find a sense of humor an important ingredient in a
man, but they never consider it is just as important to men.
To be able to find the amusing in every aspect of life is a gift
that more should cultivate. A sense of humor goes a long
way for setting a man at ease. It is captivating because it is
contagious. Contagious and outrageous, laughter just feels

good. It is healing, releasing, and can be conspiratorial in nature, binding you together, especially if the joke is only between the two of you.

Laughter is also good for the soul. It can make an ordinary face look beautiful. It can make a person with a threatening persona appear approachable. Laughter signals that people don't take themselves too seriously and cancels out needless insecurities. To be able to laugh at yourself, as well as anything entertaining, is attractive to those on the outside looking in. It says that you are at ease with yourself as well as with life in general.

A twinkle in your eye is inviting to a man. It causes their curiosity to rise. What is the secret behind that smile? Especially if they're the source of it. I recall years ago going out to dinner with a group of friends. I found one of the men there rather interesting. He had a great sense of humor and had the wittiest things to say. Little did I realize that I was the only one laughing at his comments. Later, he pursued me quite ardently until he captured my heart. When I asked him what was it about me that had piqued his interest, he replied without thinking, "You laughed at my jokes. It made me feel special, and I wanted to keep that feeling."

Women have the amazing gift of instinctively knowing how to make men see the lighter side of life. Use it well. Laughter is a welcome escape from things that can weigh a man down.

As I've said before, men fall in love with you based on how they feel when they are with you, so fill their time with laughter and good feelings. The type of feelings that make them thirst for your presence and keep them coming back for more.

Soft Tones

A gentle answer turns away wrath, but a harsh word stirs up anger (Proverbs 15:1).

*T*hough we are not opera singers, women have the amazing capacity to scale several octaves in their speaking range when they get excited or aggravated. Ssssshh! Bring it down. Remember, men talk bass. A high soprano voice can affect them adversely, especially in moments of anger or excitement.

Ahh, but a request softly spoken will most always get a response. I personally have put into practice waiting until I can calmly speak on matters that perturb me before broaching the offense with a man. Why? Perhaps it's a "mother thing," but the moment a man thinks he's being scolded or corrected, he shuts down and retreats. Never use the words, "I have to talk to you" or "we need to talk," unless you want to watch him disappear for an indefinite amount of time. Try to watch your tone. You do not want him to have to work up the courage to hear what you have to say. You also do not want to remind him of his mother—this is not romantic. Season your conversation with soft tones.

In the book of Esther, the queen had a rather urgent request. One that I am sure would have rendered me to breathless hysteria, yet she calmly waited until the king asked her what was on her mind. Then she quietly stated her case. He responded to her immediately because he was not put off by her approach. Though her problem was major, this girlfriend maintained her composure and got what she wanted from the king. In the same way, there is a way to get his attention and keep it long enough to get the results you desire.

Once a man notices that you are not prone to passionate outbursts, he will not flinch or flee when he sees you coming. Rather, he will welcome you, knowing that you are a reasonable woman who is able to rationally vocalize whatever is on your mind...so take a deep breath and speak softly.

"How was your day?"

(A little bit of interest goes a long way.)

Options

"If it pleases the king," she said (Esther 8:5).

Have you ever wondered why every time you asked the man in your life to do something, it seemed he either took his time doing it or he disappeared and didn't do it at all? I finally figured this one out after much searching and questioning of my male friends. Blame it on independent women, but men these days feel as if they are being *told* what to do, and they don't like it. They feel out of control, as if they have no options.

Want to get a man to do something for you? Position your request as a *request* and not as a *directive*. "Can you?" seems to go a long way, as well as, "What do you think is the best way to handle this?" Ooh, they really like that! You see, men are fixers. If you come up with the solution, then there is nothing left for them to fix. Most dig in their heels in defiance until they can once again gain some control and do things on their terms.

Remember, this is a book about how to get and keep a man's attention. Some of these little tidbits call for major re-arranging of our mindset as well as our independent habits. But trust me, they work. Want a man who is willing to ful-fill your heart's desire? Give him the freedom and the op-tion to do so.

Delight

*M*en like women who can find delight in the little things. Delight is something often lost in the transition from girlhood to womanhood and sometimes misconstrued as naïveté, yet it is an endearing quality that touches the heart and disarms the mind. It is that missing ingredient that makes a man want to be creative in his pursuit of seeing your eyes light up. It is the lasting memory he carries until the next time he sees you. A light that causes him to want to see you sooner than later. Take the time to enjoy a mo-ment, a comment, or a gesture, no matter how small. Watch his delight in the fact that, in your eyes, he is one of the sources that makes your heart smile.

Contentment

$\mathcal{S}$peaking of making your heart smile…What do we gain from making a man feel that he is an active ingredient in our state of contentment? A lot! The relief a man feels with the knowledge that he does not have to continually perform to make you happy releases him to love you. To love you because you are affirming and accepting. To love you because you are simply you, content and secure…no pressure…purely because you allow him to just be.

"What do you think?"

(Words that are always welcome.)

Negotiations

$\mathcal{A}$ man is drawn to a woman who knows how to work with him and not against him, regardless of his faults. Everything is subject to being worked out. For every problem, there is a solution. The woman who adds to the problem with criticism and negativity destroys the house of love she could be building by redirecting her attitude to one of openness and reasonable conversation. Listen, hear him out, make him feel heard, and then give your opinion when asked for it. Ask questions, like "How can I help you to understand what I need?" if the problem is in regard to your relationship. "What do you think is a good solution to this problem?" Listen and really hear before stating your case. Do not concentrate on delivering your script. It might change based on what he says. A man is more willing to listen if he feels you are willing to consider his ways, his feelings, his heart.

Insisting on your way will get you your way—alone. Be flexible. Search for common ground and then invite him to join you.

Silence

Your beauty should not come from outward adornment, such as braided hair and the wearing of gold jewelry and fine clothes. Instead, it should be that of your inner self, the unfading beauty of a gentle and quiet spirit, which is of great worth in God's sight (1 Peter 3:3-4).

It has been said that silence is golden, but silence is also effective. As we learn to allow men to be who they are, not demanding more than they are capable of giving, many will come into their own and give you the credit at a later date. As I sat listening to the fiancé of a friend relating when he knew he was in love, he ended his dissertation by saying, "The thing that got me about her was that she never gave up on me." That spoke more loudly to him than all the things she had done or said. Her silent presence and support in his life, as she watched him wrestle with his own issues, caused him to see a beauty in her that was greater than what his eyes could behold. A quiet and supportive spirit promised him volumes of a life filled with unconditional love.

We are women, so we can all agree that at times we talk too much—to no avail. We quickly proclaim all that we think and know. Besides, it's all true and it's all good, isn't it? But maybe our silence could speak louder to the heart of a man and challenge him in ways that we never could vocally. Could it be that silence can be more inviting than we know? Perhaps it is time to be quiet and allow silence to have its perfect work.

36
Whispers

He stilled the storm to a whisper; the waves of the sea were hushed (Psalm 107:29).

Funny thing about a whisper. You have to come closer in order to hear. And isn't that the objective? Drawing a man closer? Closer to your heart? Don't let loud speaking spoil the effect of your words or drown out what you really want him to hear.

"Ssssh!" Isn't it amazing that in the midst of a crowded and noisy room one person making this sound can bring conversations to a halt and direct all eyes to the source?

Never underestimate the power of a whisper and its ability to quiet the storm in a man.

Desire

$\mathcal{E}$very man, no matter how secure, no matter how many material trappings he possesses, longs to know that he is wanted. Desired by you. Not blatantly, as is the manner of forward and aggressive women, but quietly, thoughtfully wanted. A simple "hello" loaded with pleasure at the sound of his voice on the other end of the phone can send his heart into orbit. Letting him know you are looking forward to seeing him, or you thought of him in the middle of the day and wondered what he was doing, will send his spirits sailing. Don't be shy. Let him know that he is a source of delight and pleasure, that you consider his presence in your life to be a gift. This is a gift he will strive to share with you often and liberally.

Music

All your robes are fragrant with myrrh and aloes and cassia; from palaces adorned with ivory the music of the strings makes you glad (Psalm 45:8).

$\mathcal{A}$hh, music. It lowers the defenses and plays in divine harmony with our hearts. Atmosphere is everything. Music causes us to search ourselves and relate to the emotions intricately hidden between its rhythms. Be careful what you play or listen to in his presence. It can set the mood or destroy the foundation for good feelings.

Music is powerful. It's been researched and said that women listen to the words; men listen to the beat, the groove. It influences their senses, has the ability to move them away from or toward you. Select the music you surround yourself with carefully. Inwardly and outwardly.

Hum to yourself. What's going on inside of you will manifest outwardly. Sing out loud. Someone will join you because music is contagious. Fill your spirit and home with song. At times, music can say what you cannot. Invite him to listen to the music of your heart.

Prayer

Therefore confess your sins to each other and pray for each other so that you may be healed (James 5:16).

$\mathcal{C}$an we talk about the bonding power of praying with a man? Prayer is intimate. Prayer is transparent. For singles, praying with a potential mate or friend keeps the relationship in the right light because prayer purifies and refocuses your attention back to God and His will for your life. For married women, prayer is a balm for your husband. You can take one another to higher levels of intimacy as you bare your hearts in prayer—loving, forgiving, and lifting one another's needs before the Father. *Prayer breaks down resistance and exposes the heart. It is the place where man and woman become spiritually naked and unashamed again.* It returns us back to the garden. To the place where we lose all self-consciousness and once again become God-conscious. As you become aware of the presence of the Lord between you, your spirits are bound by an invisible third cord that cannot be broken.

A prayerful woman refreshes the spirit of a man, bringing him joy and a sense of divine peace. As I have said before, a man falls in love with a woman based on how he feels when he is with her. Under the canopy of your prayers, a man believes his heart can rest in your hands. If he knows it's safe, most likely he won't take it back.

"I love you."

(Never let this go unsaid.)

Whispers from his heart...

Amidst the clamor of the world outside,

one soft voice is heard

stilling my heart

quieting my inner man

causing me to rise above the din...

Spirit calling unto spirit

I follow its leading,

hunting for

a sanctuary

where I can place my heart for safekeeping.

It is at your invitation that I come,

trusting your promise

of an oasis.

As I wander through

the desert of my longings

in search of a

respite for my soul,

you haunt me with your endearments,

and I hope against hope

that you will let me stay

inside your spirit,

where your love

is music to my ears...

The Emotions

Smell

The Spirit

The Scent of a Woman

*So Delilah said to Samson, "Tell me the secret of
your great strength and how you can be tied up
and subdued"* (Judges 16:6).

Delilah was a bad, bad girl but we can glean price-
less information from a woman who indeed
sapped a man of his strength for the wrong reason.
Delilah, according to the Jewish historian Josephus, was a
harlot living among the Philistines. With this information in
mind, we can safely conclude her devices. She assaulted all
of Samson's senses until he surrendered the secret of his
strength to her. That man had no idea what hit him, only
that he was hooked.

Devious women of Delilah's day left no stone unturned
when appealing to men. They knew the strength of a man
is his heart. They cultivated their outer beauty with alluring
adornment. They also washed and anointed themselves
with fragrant oils that lured men to them and lingered in
the air long after their departure. They burned incense and
intoxicated their prey with sumptuous surroundings, perfumed linens, and scented candles. Add delectable meals
and full-bodied wines to the mix, along with a healthy
heaping of feigned or real admiration and praise followed
by sexual favors, and that man was total mush!

Let me once again clarify that these tactics done outside of the marriage union are not lasting. If you manage to get that duped man to the altar, you will still have great issues with trust—lingering shadows and regrets that are totally unnecessary according to God's design. Most men feel that if they seduced you so easily, others can too. Maintaining a standard of purity before marriage sets the foundation for trust and security in the future. However, God is not opposed to married couples enjoying the fullness of love and even urges the man to be intoxicated with the love that comes from the wife of his youth.

What am I saying? That the scent of a woman goes a long way in attracting the attention of a man, or in keeping the one you have once he has committed to the marriage union with you. So let's look at another area that may go overlooked or taken for granted—the sense of smell.

Cleanliness

One day Naomi her mother-in-law said to her, "My daughter, should I not try to find a home for you, where you will be well provided for? Is not Boaz, with whose servant girls you have been, a kinsman of ours? Tonight he will be winnowing barley on the threshing floor. Wash and perfume yourself, and put on your best clothes" (Ruth 3:1-3).

The nose is a sensitive thing. Smells are important because they have the power to attract or repel. They can turn one on or off. Our body scent says a lot about us—it remains even after we are gone. It is an invisible announcement of who we are. Therefore, take note of your personal scent and administer care to your body with great attention.

Perfume

How delightful is your love, my sister, my bride! How much more pleasing is your love than wine, and the fragrance of your perfume than any spice! (Song of Songs 4:10).

In days of old, women used concentrated oils for lasting fragrance, to ensure they maintained a pleasant smell even after trekking through the desert sun.

Today, scent is another category where less is always more. Choose your fragrance carefully, something that complements your natural odor (everyone has one based on their diet) and apply to clean skin. When I was a little girl, my mother always told me that applying perfume to an unwashed body was like putting icing on gingerbread—the edge of the flavor still bit through the sweetness. Your perfume should complement your natural scent and round it out with pleasing allure.

Apply just enough to make a man want to come closer and leaves an impression after you have left his presence. Familiarity and consistency with your fragrance is also a well-kept secret. Select a perfume that will be unique and foreign from what everyone else is wearing. Your scent should set you apart in his mind and form exclusive memories of you and you alone.

> *Pleasing is the fragrance of your perfumes; your name is like perfume poured out* (Song of Songs 1:3).

A man once told me that his girlfriend wore a memorable fragrance that he really loved. Whenever he was elsewhere and encountered a smell that was reminiscent of what she wore, it made him think of her and long to be in her presence. Fragrance was the conduit of pleasant feelings and memories for him. An old perfume commercial ended with a man singing, "Your Windsong stays on my mind..." Get the picture? Men have a heightened sense of smell because it affects their libido.

Single women need to be mindful of a scent's effect and take care to not send the wrong signals to the man in their life. Though you cannot control the way a man thinks, you can control your signals. Reserve setting the atmosphere for intimacy until after marriage. Do not allow memories of you to be ones filled with feelings of frustration. Married ladies, pay attention and be sensitive to the smells that affect your husband positively. Scents can leave a silent but powerful impression on his mind that will haunt him with promises of more of you. Wear them well.

Good Breath

Fresh breath is a must, especially if you want to be kissed. Your breath carries life in it. It speaks of the woman within. Fresh breath is not only inviting and pleasant, it allows closeness and intimacy without offense. Breath is internal. It can betray you if you eat things that don't contribute to its sweetness. Onions and garlic are not the only offenders. Different combinations of food that stay in our system surface in our breath. With this in mind, small wonder internal breath capsules are now on the market. Internal breath fresheners, mints, oral care strips...all of these point to the same conclusion. Fresh breath can hinder or promote a sweet exchange.

Clean Hair

Your head crowns you like Mount Carmel. Your hair is like royal tapestry; the king is held captive by its tresses (Song of Songs 7:5).

You've got to keep your head together. It is the first thing people take note of. Unkempt hair will make eyes wander in the midst of conversation and distract from all your other positive features. Short, long, or in-between, the smell and look of clean hair catches a man's eye. Select the message you want to send and then toss those locks!

Fragrant Surroundings

Obviously, the world is onto something. Scented candles, incense, and perfumed oil burners abound on the market. The power of scent is obvious. Everyone wants to stay in a room that smells good. Aromatherapy has taught us that certain smells create certain moods—relaxed, calm, or romantic notions. Select your scents with discretion.

Incense

Perfume and incense bring joy to the heart (Proverbs 27:9).

Scents set the atmosphere and make a house feel like a home. They add a feminine touch and a soft beauty that is unspeakable. Scented candles add a soft glow and illuminate not only the beauty of your home but softly perfume the air. Incense, like romance, lends a presence to a room that lingers long after it is finished burning. These are subtle touches that make a man envision what your home together would be like, or they paint memories that make him long to return home as soon as possible. And that, my friend, is a step in the right direction...

Home Cooking

"If it pleases the king," replied Esther, "let the king, together with Haman, come today to a banquet I have prepared for him." "Bring Haman at once," the king said, "so that we may do what Esther asks." So the king and Haman went to the banquet Esther had prepared (Esther 5:4-5).

Men are complaining, ladies. Women don't cook anymore, and they want to know why. Many of us are from the last generation who had mothers who cooked on a regular basis. The smell of a home-cooked meal signaled that someone you loved was waiting for you. It made you look forward to tasting what they had prepared. The kitchen was a place of security for most as children. It was the place you could always find the one who loved you unconditionally. Who nurtured you at the end of a long day. Men expect us to know how to care for them, especially by feeding and nurturing their bodies with stick-to-the-ribs fare.

I can tell you as a witness—there is truth to the rumor that the way to a man's heart is through his stomach. So be careful whom you cook for. Just kidding! If a queen, as in Esther, could get her husband king to drop affairs of state and run off to a banquet that she had prepared for him, just think what you can accomplish with a good meal. The meal that Esther prepared for the king inspired him to come to her aid and defend her very life.

Something happens when you serve someone food made with your own hands. It is not just an expression of servanthood—it is an impartation of your spirit to theirs. They are aware of the effort taken to do a special service just for them. As the food warms their inner man, it also warms their heart toward you. For further insight on this topic, I highly recommend *God Is in the Kitchen Too* by P.B. Wilson. In the meantime, don't feel condemned over this issue. It is normal not to enjoy something you don't understand, like cooking, or feel uncomfortable doing it because you lack the needed knowledge. Here is my suggestion: When you taste something you like, ask the person who prepared it to show you how they made it. A repertoire of seven simple meals is all you need to get you started on your culinary way.

Remember, the dinner table is a place of offering, communion, and fellowship. It is through fellowship that secrets are whispered and intimacy is deepened. It is the place where heartfelt emotions are revealed, positive changes are made, and commitments are birthed. The smell of cooking will lead a man home. So turn up the flame, girl!

> *There is no sight on earth more appealing than the sight of a woman making dinner for someone she loves.*
>
> —Thomas Wolfe

An inside look at scent...

Truly the natural air and scents around you are one thing, but the spirit is also sensitive to smell. *A funky attitude* or *a putrid disposition* are phrases we throw around without realizing how true they are. It is time to look inward and learn of the smells that others might sense but you do not intellectually detect. *The invisible reveals more about you than you know to others in your midst*—particularly to a man who will be hypersensitive to anything you give off. One of the smelliest books of the Bible is Song of Songs, known for its passionate romantic dissertation. If there were ever two people more aware of smell as well as taste, it was the Shulammite and her beloved. For greater insight into cultivating lasting romance, let's take a look at the power and the smell of the fruit we bear.

Inner Purity and Godliness

A funky outward attitude tells the story of what is deep within. The adverse winds of life, or storms encountered in relationships, should not fill the air with an unpleasing odor. Rather, they should reveal your inner woman. *Your garden should be filled with the fruit of the Spirit, causing a sweet scent to emanate from you.* Harsh words, silent treatments, mood swings, and attitudes that cause a man to want to keep his distance should not be present.

Gardens in Scripture signified entering into kingdom living—a place where righteousness, peace, and joy resided. The garden was all about pleasurable living, seclusion from the outside world, a sanctuary, an oasis.

Be an oasis, a place to water the soul of a man because your spirit has a predisposition to do so. It is already full of the goodness of God and free of insecurity, past baggage, unforgiveness, and wrong ideas and attitudes toward men. You must be free enough inside yourself to allow every man to rise or fall on his own merit. If you are not there, I recommend taking a sabbatical from the dating game to tend your own garden.

Though married women cannot take sabbaticals from their husbands, they must find ways to nurture the fruit of their spirit. Making sure they spend quiet time with the Lord and have healthy exchanges with friends who lend wise counsel. They need to have open communication with their husbands where they can deal with the feelings they may struggle with in their marriage. When you have been cultivated and freed from all debilitating undergrowth, when your flowers are in full bloom along with your heart, then feel free to invite someone in to enjoy the bouquet.

Sweetness

Pleasant words are as an honeycomb, sweet to the soul, and health to the bones (Proverbs 16:24 KJV).

*H*oney was used in Scripture to signify abundance. Thick, rich, and golden, it clings to where it is placed. So do your words. Sweet words leave a sweet scent in the air for the listener that cling to his spirit long after they have been spoken.

Milk and Honey

*W*ords, like milk and honey, can be nourishing. Smooth and rich, comforting and promoting rest. Your words can change the countenance of a man and change the complexion of your relationship. Milk is necessary in the life of an infant, promoting growth. Honey sweetens the taste and increases the appetite for more. Your words also hold the power of life and death. They can promote your relationship to higher heights and deeper depths of love or destroy your romance. There is an art to speaking into the heart of your man and penetrating his spirit. Words well placed have a lasting effect, so select what you say wisely.

Choice Fruits

*H*ave you ever entered a room where a bowl of fruit has been left on the table? The air is pungent and rich with the promise of good things. Small wonder so many scented candles are flavored with fruit scents. They whet your appetite for the taste. One bite into any piece of succulent fruit produces pleasure and refreshment. Sweet to the taste, not only does fruit nourish you, it cleanses your system. It is good for you! Perhaps this is why you can never eat too much...

> *But the fruit of the Spirit is love, joy, peace, patience, kindness, goodness, faithfulness, gentleness and self-control. Against such things there is no law* (Galatians 5:22-23).

A sure dessert you can serve to a man and know it will always be a success is fruit. The same is true of the fruit of the Spirit. No one will ever get enough of love, joy, peace, patience, kindness, goodness, faithfulness, gentleness, and self-control. Be liberal with your servings and see your vineyard blossom and flourish. Romance will ripen in fertile ground where only good things grow.

Frankincense

*I*n order to understand the value of scents, one must first understand their properties. Frankincense, one of the gifts presented to Jesus at His birth, was gathered and used as incense as well as being an ingredient in sacred anointing oil. It was used in sacrificial offerings as well as for perfume. It was considered an exotic scent and very valuable. Just as frankincense represents the ultimate sacrifice, the question must be asked, how selfless are you? A man can sense when everything is "all about you." Be willing to be sacrificial. In the end, you have nothing to lose and everything to gain.

Myrrh

I arose to open for my lover, and my hands dripped with myrrh, my fingers with flowing myrrh, on the handles of the lock (Song of Songs 5:5).

Myrrh is extracted from a tree that bears little white flowers as well as fruit. In biblical times, myrrh was a very valuable article of trade. It was used for embalming the dead, in the purification rites for women, in anointing oil, and in perfume. It was also thought of as a labdanum and was mingled with wine and served to Jesus during the crucifixion.

A woman must carry herself with an air that expresses attributes of being able and willing to sacrifice at the appropriate times for love. However, she should never spiritualize catering to a man who is abusive or selfish. Both partners must be willing to bend and give for the sake of the other. Though being selfless is a valuable and rare trait, this type of attitude can only come from a pure heart.

Be willing to let go of your idea of how everything should be between the two of you. Purify your thinking and attitudes and remain open to the possibilities that he wants to present. Listen and then lift and separate what has been shared. Embrace the better parts of what he offers to sweeten your relationship.

A woman must also be willing to revive the spirits of her man and soothe his wounded places. She must be able to administer the oil of comfort when needed to preserve his confidence and state of well-being. It is in the midst of the healing aroma of a woman's comfort that a man is finally able to rest.

Fruit, Nard, and Saffron

Your plants are an orchard of pomegranates with choice fruits, with henna and nard, nard and saffron, calamus and cinnamon, with every kind of incense tree, with myrrh and aloes and all the finest spices (Song of Songs 4:13-14).

*W*hat you manifest outwardly comes from within. Make sure your fruit is not common fare but rare, succulent offerings with endless possibilities of discovering a new delightful flavor. Pomegranates were known for being hard on the outside but filled with sweet fruit on the inside that could be eaten raw or made into spiced wine. Today's society makes women feel they must muster a tough exterior.

Perhaps in some cases that is true, but you must never allow your inner woman to harden. Preserve your softness and your sweetness so the right man may partake of all you have to offer.

Nard was an expensive oil that was used as a liquid or made into an ointment. It was most often stored and only used to anoint a special or honored guest. The man in your life should always feel special. Truly he can smell when he is being treated like everyone else and feel devalued. Never should a whiff of commonness pass between you. Keep him set apart in your heart.

Just as crocus blooms were gathered, dried, and pressed into cakes of saffron, your attentions must be gathered to focus on the one you desire to be special in your life. And just as saffron was used to color various dishes, your attitude will color the tone of your relationship with your significant other. Sprinkle attention and caring as liberally as saffron was spread, as perfume, on the floors for weddings in the days of old. Soft and inviting, so the scent of affection in the air is not overdone.

Calamus and Cinnamon

Some fruit does not give away its scent until it is crushed, like the calamus. Our hearts are similar when faced with disappointment in relationships. Keep your sweet savor. Do not allow past wounds to sour your perfume or your disposition. Blend cinnamon and calamus together as the apothecary did in order to add it to your own personal anointing oil that is unique to your life and experiences. Massage yourself with hope for the future. Trust me, a man can smell past pain just as he can detect the scent of openness to love.

Aloe

*A*loes are known for their healing properties—their preservative powers as well as their perfume. Take the time to heal yourself and revel in your own wholeness. Let the aroma of your heart be a healing agent in a man's life. This is a scent that will cause his heart to be at rest in your hands.

Wine

May your breasts be like the clusters of the vine, the fragrance of your breath like apples, and your mouth like the best wine. May the wine go straight to my lover, flowing gently over lips and teeth (Song of Songs 7:8-9).

*W*ine is tested by its smell or "bouquet." Potent, sweet, light, or dry, the hint is in the aroma. Your conversation can intoxicate a man—master the art of it. Mellow and rich, spicy and interesting, it should always leave him thirsty for yet another conversation with you. Share from your heart tidbits that tickle his ears and cause him to reflect later on what you said. The scent of a good discussion should linger, go down smoothly into his spirit, and leave a warm and pleasant feeling in the center of his core.

Never fall into the habit of being predictable. Mix it up. Wisdom combined with mystery, or romantic little sayings sprinkled with honor. Your relationship should become richer, mellower, and more full-bodied with time. Slowly pour your affection in portions not greater than the vessel's ability to hold it. Pace yourself in your offerings. Love is to be savored in little sips, making the flavor last longer.

Mandrakes

The mandrakes send out their fragrance, and at our door is every delicacy, both new and old, that I have stored up for you, my lover (Song of Songs 7:13).

Dark, sweet, fragrant, and abundant, mandrakes had a narcotic quality that was used at times as a love potion and other times medicinally. A woman's love can be a powerful drug to a man. Heady, stimulating, causing his senses to swim, healing him within. It is the secret things that stir a man within. The sweet, thoughtful things done and said, stored up for only him, leave thoughts of you like perfume permeating his senses, breaking through his concentration in the middle of the day. They put more pleasurable thoughts on his mind as respites in the midst of everyday frenzy. A single man tends to commit when a single woman leaves him wanting more. These are also the things that make a married man look forward to going home at the end of a hard day's work.

Apples and Raisins

Strengthen me with raisins, refresh me with apples, for I am faint with love (Song of Songs 2:5).

$\mathcal{G}$rapes are a versatile fruit that can be eaten fresh, made into wine, or dried into raisins. Raisins have an enduring quality that gets sweeter as they age. And apples were often spoken of figuratively to portray how precious we are to God. Enduring and precious, two words that should always be companions to love. Truly a woman's love strengthens a man. The promise of your enduring love gives him the impetus to keep on keeping on. The knowledge that one he finds precious also holds him in the same esteem is food for his soul. He is a man possessed. The scent of confidence a man wears when he knows his woman is behind him is unmistakable to all who encounter him.

Garden Fountain

You are a garden locked up, my sister, my bride; you are a spring enclosed, a sealed fountain (Song of Songs 4:12).

$\mathcal{S}$ecret delights hide behind garden walls, but the scent of flowers betray their presence. Flowing fountains cool the air and give it a sense of freshness that does not exist beyond its wall. This is a place one would have to visit in order to find this particular array of pleasing aromas. A private place where only those who have the key can enter.

The garden is your body, kept pure and secluded from the affections and visits of other passersby. Locked and awaiting this one special man's arrival. Once married, it offers not only a place of refuge, but untouched waters that are his alone for drinking and partaking of your refreshing love and affections.

Longings from his soul...

There is a scent in the air

promises of love

soft and alluring

calling me

to come out of myself

and into your heart...

and though I fear

losing the man that I am,

the man that I am bound to become

with you

smells sweeter,

and so I follow the aroma

of your spirit

that pulls me

deeper and deeper

into your heart.

Never looking back

I am led captive

by your perfume,

finding myself

immersed

in all that is you

still praying

that you are not

a mere vapor

too good

to be true...

The Physical

Taste

The Spirit

The Spice of Life

A woman flavors a man's world like no other spice, causing explosions in his emotions as well as his physical self. He responds to all that she is. Hot, cold, sweet, bitter, sometimes downright salty (as in a definite edge to her personality)! Your encounter with a man can leave him with sweet memories or a bitter aftertaste in his mouth. Though some tastes must be acquired, few like to experiment with so delicate a sense, therefore, make sure yours is pleasing to the palate of his heart. Check yourself and what you're serving up. It could determine if love will be on the menu or not.

Refreshing

You are a garden fountain, a well of flowing water streaming down from Lebanon (Song of Songs 4:15).

*A*mazing how many times in Scripture women were found beside a well before they met their husbands. *Could it be that God fashioned women to be sources of refreshment for men?* I believe so. A hand extended promises to soothe a weary brow. Laughter, as magical as the sound of a brook, chases away the cares of the day. Eyes that shine with love and admiration reveal the depths of your heart and invite your husband to come closer to partake of all the refreshment you have to offer.

Your mystery is your greatest lure, causing a man to venture closer and look deeper still. Once he has committed his life to you in marriage, allow him to drink continually from your well, until he is satisfied and refreshed.

Moods

I the LORD do not change (Malachi 3:5).

*M*oodiness can flavor a relationship with bitterness or sweetness. Moods are interesting things: subtle, changing, and shifting according to the weather, circumstances, health, and the actions of others. Moods can be either good, bad, or indifferent. However, they can also be intriguing if your moods are pleasant ones.

No one can always be in a good mood, but it is important to aim for consistency. Moody women throw men off balance. They don't feel safe. God speaks of one of His attributes as being unchanging, so it must be an important virtue. We always know what to expect from God—He is consistently holy, loving, and good.

Moodiness can season your relationship with uncertainty. Uncertainty leaves the door open for confusion between parties, and confusion can only lead to the demise of anything you were trying to build with the man of your dreams.

So change your clothes, change your hair—you can even change your mind—but keep shifting moods to a minimum.

Tears

Thou hast taken account of my wanderings; Put my tears in Thy bottle (Psalm 56:8 NASB).

There is something so tender about the image of God collecting our tears in a bottle. Because the heart of a man is fashioned after God, one must believe that a woman's tears touch a tender place in the heart of most men as well. Salty tears stir them to cover a woman to protect her. To be her problem solver. To be the dashing knight in shining armor in her world. Tears bring a different flavor to your interaction. They season the atmosphere with tenderness. With loving concern. A deeper level of protectiveness.

However, crocodile tears do not qualify. Most men know when they are being manipulated, and they resent it. But they also have a hard time with a woman who sports false bravado. In other words, be your authentic self. When you hurt, it's okay to say ouch and allow him the privilege of being there for you.

Fears

Perfect love drives out fear (1 John 4:18).

Feeling fearful? Let him into that place with you. Let him see the things that frighten you. Make him responsible for your heart, and he will take care of it. If you build a wall to protect your own heart and emotions, watch him abdicate his responsibility. Don't be confused. Though the Bible tells us to guard our hearts with all diligence, the principle is that you should shield your heart in the sense that you are careful and discerning of who deserves close proximity. However, if he has earned your trust, then by all means be open, transparent, and revealing.

A man needs to be your knight in shining armor. It is part of his very nature. Rob him of this, and his heart will grow restless and begin to search for something or someone who allows him to be all he was created to be. Allow him to cover you, to love you, and chase your fears away. Let him be your hero and fulfill his own need to be there for you.

Secrets

A gift given in secret soothes anger (Proverbs 21:14).

Secrets are binding. They make a man feel he has access to a place in your heart that no one else does. In a sense, you give power to the person who is entrusted with your secrets. Empower your man. Inspire him to use his power wisely, which he will if he feels he has your trust. Again, you must leave room for a man to rise to the occasion. Give him something to work with. Allow him to feel that he is truly a part of you.

Trust makes people responsible. Give him responsibility. *Things spoken in secret allows him to know that you have confidence in his ability to keep a part of you that is sacred.* Make him the keeper of something in your world, and he will assume his post with diligence.

Now a word of caution: This does not mean that you tell him the sordid details of your past and mistakes you are ashamed of. God has thrown those things into the sea of forgetfulness, and you should not go fishing. However, if something from your past will affect your future with this man, then wait for the appropriate time (which is after he has committed himself to you) to carefully share only the details he needs to know. Many women feel the need to spill all the beans long before the man has made a heart decision toward them, and they find themselves in dismay when he vacates the scene. Remember that love covers a multitude of sins. If love isn't there, he will not have the capacity to handle your past. Share the secret places of yourself, but carefully choose what you share. Make sure that what you confide binds and does not separate.

Dreams

Two are better than one because they have a good reward for their labor (Ecclesiastes 4:9 KJV).

Let him be a partner with you in your dreams. Set goals together. In this world where independence is applauded, many men feel as if they are on the outside looking in. Don't just harbor your dreams, share them. Allow him to be your lighthouse, guiding you toward your destination. The taste of mutual success is sweet. Make him a part of your success, and he will applaud you. Leave him outside of your aspirations, and he will resent your accomplishments.

In the same fashion, encourage his dreams and partner with him in them. Dreams, like secrets, are conspiratorial in nature. They bind two people together. Remember that a helpmeet is a woman who is equipped with everything her man needs to help him complete his God-given assignment in life. Single and married women alike must be cognizant of this and learn to have the man in their life share his dreams. This is an important component of friendship as well as courtship. As you fill that slot in his life, his heart will be drawn to you—the woman who helps him make his dreams come true. Be his dreamweaver, cultivate his dreams to life, blend your touch into the fabric of his deepest longings. This is the secret to remaining the woman of his dreams.

Needs

Then the king said to her, "What is troubling you, Queen Esther? And what is your request? Even to half of the kingdom it will be given to you" (Esther 5:3 NASB).

If it is true a man needs to feel needed by you, then surely you must let him know your needs. This is scary, but necessary, in any relationship that moves forward. Remember, he's not a mindreader. Don't expect him to guess what you want. Your needs must be palpable to him. He needs to be able to sink his teeth into them, digest them, and be able to offer you a solution. Make him feel he is a part of you by sharing your needs with him. Allow him to answer them.

Pick your battles, ladies. Don't overwhelm him by expecting too much too soon. Be gentle and present your needs in a way he can receive them. Make him feel as if you are asking for help. *Submit* your need to him. Do not make demands or unrealistic requirements that cause him to shut down emotionally or flee.

Stay watchful and listen to his conversation. Ask him what he needs from you. Learn of his needs and address them. A man's heart is warmed when he feels you truly care about the things on his heart.

Be quick to acknowledge when he has met your needs—it will encourage him to look for other ways to please you. When a man knows he is meeting your needs, it makes him feel empowered. And a woman who makes a man feel powerful is a woman he will want to be around.

Goodness

$\mathcal{B}$e a treasure chest loaded with deliciously good things. An endless supply of pleasant surprises.

Put a smile on his face in the middle of the day as he remembers your goodness.

> Understanding,
>> Kind,
>
> Fun,
>> And oh so good...

Accentuate the positive in your personality and abilities. If you always put your best face forward, it is what he will remember. Though none of us are perfect, let the good memories outnumber the bad.

Wisdom

$\mathcal{A}$ man looks for a woman who not only stimulates his mind but adds the flavor of wisdom to his world. Your wisdom holds the key to him possessing honor, success, power, long life, and wealth—not just materially, but spiritually and emotionally as well. You, like the Proverbs 31 woman, are instrumental in him gaining respect among his peers.

Be well informed. Acquire knowledge. Gain understanding. Be a wellspring of good suggestions and worthy advice, offering them when appropriate. Don't lecture, teach, or preach. Draw him out and share things for him to consider. Allow him the privilege of making wise choices, and then praise him for doing so.

Keep in mind that a wise woman never flaunts her wisdom; she equips others to feel wise.

Creativity

In the beginning God created the heaven and the earth (Genesis 1:1).

One of the most incredible attributes we have inherited from our heavenly Father is the gift of creativity. A woman has the natural ability to take nothing and turn it into something beautiful. Use this gift wisely to create smiles, good feelings, and confidence in your man. Add a splash of red somewhere unexpected. A flower to a vacant space. Take a scarf and turn it into a wall hanging or a skirt.

Perhaps inventiveness is a better word—using what you have and making it into something greater. Creativity is like a gourmet meal—it is the various flavors of your personality that can be savored bite by bite, an experience at a time. A simple dish can become gourmet because of the way you arrange it on the plate. Every woman must learn to master this. A man takes note and harbors secret pride about this facet of your being. You become a woman he wants to show off to his friends because you are able to make the mundane special. Be your own Martha Stewart. Collect witty ideas and creative inventions, and then take them up a notch with your own personal touch. Now, stand back and admire your handiwork the way God did, and invite your man to celebrate your creation.

Resourcefulness

She looks for wool and flax, and works with her hands in delight (Proverbs 31:13 NASB).

$\mathcal{M}$y friends laugh at me because I will massage something until I've squeezed every drop of usefulness out of it. If a pair of pants is no longer fitting the way I want them to fit, I will take them to a seamstress, have her open the legs, and make them into a skirt. In my mind, why waste perfectly good fabric? They call it creative. I call it resourceful. A little bit of that goes a long way with a man as he observes how you handle yourself in everyday living. Single and married men want to know if you will waste his hard-earned money or be a good steward of what he makes available to you. Better yet, will you be resourceful with it if the need arises?

> *She considers a field and buys it; from her earnings she plants a vineyard* (Proverbs 31:16 NASB).

Every man wants a woman who is resourceful in her own right. Creative in the way she maintains herself as well as being able to supply the needs of others. In these financially chaotic times, helplessness and irresponsibility are not attractive features for a long-term relationship. It is all hands on deck. That does not mean every woman has to be a working woman; she merely must be resourceful where she is—in business or at home. Stay informed and keep your eye out for good investments. Add to his life. Do not subtract. Equip yourself with the understanding you need to make a contribution.

> *She is not afraid of the snow for her household,*
> *for all her household are clothed with scarlet.*
> *She makes coverings for herself; her clothing is*
> *fine linen and purple* (Proverbs 31:21-22 NASB).

Can you cope and make things stretch in times of emergency? How well do you work with what you have? Watch how you spend your money now and determine if you need to change your ways in order to become an asset to the man in your life. Believe me, he is going to flee if he sees you as a liability. On the other hand, the more he can trust you with, the more he will give to you. A man wants to know that not only is his heart safe with you, but so is his wallet.

Passion

He gave them these orders: "You must serve faithfully and wholeheartedly in the fear of the LORD" (2 Chronicles 19:9).

*A*re you with him or not? That is the question on his heart. Not just in the passionate sense that is associated with lust or physical intimacy. Passion must begin before this can occur. Feeling deeply convicted about being in his corner. Being fully determined to reach the goals and aspirations you've made together or individually. Passion is the pepper in the dish of life—it makes it spicy. Nothing is sexier than a woman who is passionate. Be passionate about life—the things that matter to you as well as your man.

A man can discern what type of lover you will be after marriage by the way you approach life and all that concerns him. Are you gung ho or passive about the things you want and desire? I'm talking about the depth of your emotions. The rivers that run deep in your soul that become fountains when the right buttons are pushed. Fully focused. Completely involved and sold out. Hmm…it seems that God and man want the same thing—passion.

> *Love the* LORD *your God with all your heart and with all your soul and with all your strength* (Deuteronomy 6:5).

I must insert a sidebar here about your love life. If you are single, examine how you feel about sex and your own sexuality. Nurture healthy attitudes about both of these before you get married. The marriage bed is not the place to work out old, buried issues. Get them resolved while you are free to do so. As your courtship enters the engagement stage, matters of intimacy must be openly discussed. If you feel that it would be a temptation to do this on your own, make sure you talk about this area in premarital counseling. The goal is clear. Be ready to enjoy the marriage experience. I've said time and time again—men like ladies in the living room and uninhibited lovers in the bedroom. You will either become the woman of his fantasies or leave room for someone else to be. God created sex and decreed it good. The marriage bed must be undefiled. It becomes the privilege of a married man and woman to thoroughly enjoy their intimate experience together.

Married ladies, be prepared mentally and spiritually to enjoy the gift of sex. To love and enjoy your body as well as his. To be passionate and giving. This is a ministry to your husband. It affirms his masculinity and crowns him as king in your inner sanctum. Let him know that you passionately desire all of him, and he will be passionate about giving you all that he has.

Love

Love is patient, love is kind. It does not envy, it does not boast, it is not proud. It is not rude, it is not self-seeking, it is not easily angered, it keeps no record of wrongs. Love does not delight in evil but rejoices with the truth. It always protects, always trusts, always hopes, always perseveres. Love never fails (1 Corinthians 13:4-8).

*T*he bottom line is men want the same thing women want...love. Someone who loves them enough to be patient and kind, to rejoice and celebrate their accomplishments. They don't want someone who is critical and touchy, suspicious and accusing. There is no room for insecurity in love. Love doesn't jump to imaginary conclusions. Though it is realistic, it always hopes for the best and is courageous enough to believe in the object of its affections.

Love makes you a lady. It nurtures trust and sets a man's heart at rest because true love is faithful and loyal. It doesn't compete with the beloved, but promotes him to be the best that he can be. In turn, you reap all of the rewards for his successes. He, in turn, feels like a king and crowns you queen.

Let him know the best thing about your love is that it grows. It is flexible. It is able to withstand storms and controversy. But most of all, it overcomes all things, including your own fears. Release yourself to love and be loved in return.

Strength

It is God who arms me with strength and makes my way perfect (Psalm 18:32).

Though a man is attracted to a woman who needs him, helplessness can be a deal breaker. Why is the delicate balance between needing him and being able to handle life on your own so important? Because he needs to know that if something happened to him, you would be able to carry on. When a man loves you, he projects into the future to prepare for real or imagined emergencies because your care and safety are of foremost concern to him. If he feels you would be in peril and his future children would not be able to be cared for properly, it gives him pause for thought when considering you to be the one for him. Strength is the meat and potatoes of a relationship. A basic ingredient needed for good nourishment and healthy living.

> *She is clothed with strength and dignity; she can laugh at the days to come* (Proverbs 31:25).

Examine yourself. Do you want a man because you are waiting to be rescued or do you really want to partner with someone in this journey we call life? Your answer could affect your love life in the future. None of the men I spoke to were interested in helpless women. The reality is: A man is looking for a partner, one who can assist him in making life better for the two of you. He does not want to have to carry the entire load of your existence, and he was not created to.

Learn to be self-sufficient without becoming totally independent. This is not a contradictory statement. It is merely a challenge to you to be capable with the issues of life, while being willing to yield the parts he wants to assume responsibility for gracefully. Just because you can do it all by yourself doesn't mean you have to. Allow him the room to care for you. But always be ready to pick up the slack if need be.

> *Strengthen the feeble hands, steady the knees that give way; say to those with fearful hearts, "Be strong, do not fear; your God will come..."* (Isaiah 34:3-4).

Vulnerability

"I am your servant Ruth," she said. "Spread the corner of your garment over me, since you are a kinsman-redeemer" (Ruth 3:9).

*D*on't mistake vulnerability for weakness. Just as meekness is strength under control, vulnerability is the capacity to unashamedly yield to your needs and make them known. Nothing pulls at a man's heartstrings more than your vulnerability. It exposes your inner being, the softer side of you, which is always appealing. It is a subtle flavor, not seen with the eye, yet you know it is there when you taste it.

There is something about someone who can simply say, "This is what I need, can you help me?" Lack of vulnerability merely reveals pride. Pride in strength you don't truly possess. An I-can-do-it-all-by-myself attitude repels those who want to be a part of your world. *Pride builds walls that no man can, or wants to, climb.* It presents a false bravado that is hard for even the most willing to penetrate. Sometimes we find ourselves trapped behind walls of pride that we no longer know how to tear down. But in order to experience true love, the walls must come down and be replaced with transparency.

Remember, the woman who allows her man to help her will go far. But the woman who insists on making it happen on her own will most likely stand alone and fail alone.

All of you, clothe yourselves with humility toward one another, because, "God opposes the proud but gives grace to the humble" (1 Peter 5:5).

Warmth

$\mathcal{T}$alking about flava! When was the last time you enjoyed anything lukewarm? It kind of kills the taste, doesn't it? Want a man to enjoy the flavor of your love? Warm it up. Warmth is a welcome thing in any friendship or marriage. Turn up the burner on your personality. Be a welcome fire for him to sit in front of, 'cause, baby, it's cold outside. When he is assaulted with the cold, hard facts of life, you should be there to thaw out his heart with warmth and comfort.

Men long to be warmed by the love of the woman in their life. Just as you keep your home warm, you must offer warmth from within. Why do men describe some women as being cold? Because they're unapproachable, offering no comfort. Looking back, men recall the warmth of their mother's embrace, the comfort it held for them being folded inside of loving arms, whispered words of assurance. The look of love on their mothers' faces…

And the warmth I'm talking about is not sexual, though it can be. I speak of the warmth that fills a room when you enter. Make that man feel better. Let him be warmed from the inside out because of your presence and your presence alone.

Childlike Innocence

$\mathcal{C}$hildren are innocent and nonpretentious. They delight in the little things without studying to be sophisticated and controlled. They simply are who they are with no apologies. Refreshingly honest and transparent. They haven't learned the art of masking their feelings yet, so no guessing games are played. They are not ashamed of their tears and can giggle with abandon at the silliest things. They are unreserved with their affections.

Forgiving. Believing all things. Forever hopeful. Playful. They feel rich with the simplest pleasures. They are easy to please. Uncomplicated. Amusing, enchanting, magical, experimental, curious...open to the endless possibilities of life. They dare to dream lofty dreams, never quenching them. And when they give themselves to a hug, they revel in it. A woman should keep a healthy portion of these attributes in her life and allow them to flavor the essence of who she is.

Why? Because inside of every man is a little boy who still likes to play. To tease, to poke, to be mischievous. Who still enjoys a good wrestling match, whether physical or mental. You must be able to relate to the child within. Go ahead and be a little girl again. Celebrate the freedom it brings. Boy meets girl...that's where the greatest romances have always begun.

78 Woman

The man said, "This is now bone of my bones and flesh of my flesh; she shall be called 'woman,' for she was taken out of man" (Genesis 2:23).

A woman who enjoys being a woman is the most desirable creature to a man. Feminine, all girl, we are a mystery to men they are determined to solve. There is something about women that men envy. You should enjoy the aspects of your femininity. It is clear to a man when you are having a good time being who you were created to be.

A real man is looking for a real woman. He recognizes one when he sees her and desires to join himself to her, knowing deep within she is the missing piece of his existence.

What happens when you abdicate your feminine ways? You become unrecognizable as the one he is searching for. Like salt and pepper flavor a dish with the perfect balance, a man and woman season one another and make life a delicious adventure that both can savor. So be womanly. Soft and strong. Vulnerable and ferocious. Dependent and powerful. Wise and childlike. Stubborn and unpredictable. A host of subtle contradictions that make you all the more fascinating and deliciously all woman.

Softness

I believe our outside reflects what is within. As we strive for firm abs and sculpted biceps, let us not get hard where it really counts—the heart.

> *I will give you a new heart and put a new spirit in you; I will remove from you your heart of stone and give you a heart of flesh* (Ezekiel 36:26).

Though many of us have been wounded and disappointed by past relationships, we must never harden our hearts or our dispositions. Forgive, release, and then forgive again. Bitterness and hardness have an unpleasant taste a man can detect a mile away, and trust me, he won't come any closer. Don't sharpen your defenses. Rather, sand your rough edges to a smoothness he will want to touch. There is a grace in a woman's softness, especially if she has weathered rough storms that strengthened her resolve to maintain who she is and not be devastated by the experience. A man senses this and moves to protect and preserve it.

Take a look around you and see what most famous male artists have always painted up to present day. Not six-pack abs, but women—round and soft. Not just outwardly. Even their countenances speak of an inner quietness and gentle beauty—tender and warm. Obviously, this is their preference.

Modesty

$\mathcal{L}$et's keep it real. There is a time and a place for everything. The bottom line is, though a married man likes a woman who is not inhibited and uptight in the bedroom, he wants a lady in every other room in the house. Remember, a man's greatest issue is that of trusting a woman. He wants to know you can keep his secrets. It is important to note that in a man's mind, his greatest secret should be his woman. Everyone should not know and see what he knows and sees about you.

In his mind, your body should be his secret sanctuary. Don't let the world see all your wares. Those are for the

eyes of your husband only. Sexy is as sexy does. This is not
a matter of clothing. Today's society is sadly mistaken as
they choose to expose more and more, abandoning all
modesty.

Recently I was sitting in an airport when three young
women walked by. It was winter, mind you, but one of the
young women had on a halter top with her midsection exposed. As she paraded back and forth, the men around me
were looking at her and frowning behind her back. She be-
came the laughingstock of the section I was sitting in.
"What is she trying to prove?" one man said. I wondered
how she would feel if she knew the responses she was
drawing. Trying hard does not go over well when attempt-
ing sexiness. Ahh…but the mystery of modesty—that is
downright intriguing! Leave others to guess and want to
know more.

Every woman should consider herself a wrapped present.
A personal gift for her mate only. To expose all that you
offer him to the scrutiny of others makes it common, no
longer special. Half the pleasure of a gift is unwrapping it.
One layer at a time builds a pleasant suspense for discovering all that lies beneath its folds. Indeed, a woman should
always flavor her husband's world with pleasant surprises
of who she is a little at a time, always leaving him wanting
to discover more of what no one else knows.

Understanding

When we finally grasp the fact that we are all the re-
cipients of God's gracious compassion, we will reflect that
to others around us. We will allow others to be themselves.

We will release them from our expectations and be more understanding. The idea of understanding is a simple one. People can only be who they are based on their experiences and exposure until they learn of God's Word, renew their minds, and allow Him to transform them. Therefore, get rid of impatient demands and unrealistic expectations; they only prove to frustrate you in the long run. They put an endless strain on a relationship and leave a bad taste in everyone's mouth.

> *But by the grace of God I am what I am* (1 Corinthians 15:10).

Stop, consider all angles, and maintain a balanced perspective when presenting issues that you are struggling with to your man. Be a woman of understanding, graciously sharing your feelings and desires, yet leave room for his answers without compromising your true feelings. He will love and respect you for it. Your respect will challenge him to be responsible and strive to be a better man because you are being gracious. As God gives us grace, we must extend it to the man in our life and leave room for him to rise to another level. Understand that he is just a man. So help a brother out and keep a little honey under your tongue.

Cries of a man's spirit...

Life has been bitter,

sweeten its taste with your spirit

stirring it slowly into my world,

warming me inwardly,

soothing my soul

like hot chocolate on a cold

and stormy night.

Draw me into you

and saturate me with your goodness...

Life has been hard to swallow.

Soothe my parched spirit

with your kindness,

honeyed and rich

with promises

that I can make it with

you by my side,

leaving sweet memories

in my mouth

of all the different flavors of you

that fill me

that satisfy me

that make me smile

in spite of the dish

life serves me.

For you, my lady,

are my dessert.

Emotion

Touch

The Soul

A Woman's Touch

We've heard so much about a woman's touch that perhaps we've begun to take for granted how powerful it can be. It's time to revisit this philosophy. We know what our physical touch can do to the opposite sex, but what about the other touches you add to his world that make a huge difference in his psyche and even his appearance? Like the way you make a house a home, the personal touch you add to everything in his world makes you unique in his eyes.

As we rush to and fro, busier than we've ever been as women, some things have been sacrificed in search of greater achievements out there in our bustling world. We've forgotten the importance of taking care of self, home, and our loved ones first. A woman's touch is not just a beautifier, it is a stabilizer to men, children, our communities, and, ultimately, the world at large. God created beauty, but it often takes a woman to notice it, nurture it, and cultivate it.

I've often said that men are like Picasso and women are like Monet. Men think in bold patches—they see the big picture, the end of the matter. Women are more attuned to details, the soft hues that add dimension to the scenery of life. Women open their senses to a vast array of pleasant surprises that often go overlooked. But these details, once

111

noticed, can change the countenance, transform a mood, and warm the heart.

Let's take a look at the ingredients for making your house an oasis for the man in your life as well as all who visit. It's been said that home is where the heart is. Make your home a place where the heart wants to remain.

Influence

A woman's touch speaks louder than any words that she can ever utter

> to the heart

>> the soul

>>> the mind...

Oh, the unspoken difference a woman's touch makes.

Home

The wise woman builds her house, but with her own hands the foolish one tears hers down (Proverbs 14:1).

*Y*our home is the expression of who you are. Furnish it with care. Each piece whispers secrets about you. From the couch to the rugs on the floor, each makes its own statement. In Africa, the philosophy is you never really know a person until you have seen their home.

What does your home say about you? Are you bold, conservative, warm, inviting, imaginative, eclectic, artistic, sensitive? Do you decorate by the book, creating a sterile existence that says nothing about who you really are, or do you add your own personal taste and touch to your surroundings? Can someone tell if you are a family person? If scenery is important to you? If you are cool or hot? Romantic or conventional? A home does not have to be expensively done to be beautiful. Take what you have and apply your imagination. The goal here is to make a house a home by adding touches that personalize your space.

Do people feel peace when they visit you or are they restless? If it takes a long time to get them to say goodbye, you have your answer. People are reluctant to leave a place where they feel surrounded by calm, warmth, and contentment.

Your home should be a blessing to others besides yourself. Inviting, clean, and beautiful. A retreat from the outside world.

Atmosphere

But as for me and my household, we will serve the LORD (Joshua 24:15).

You set the tone in your home. How do you want your man to feel when he walks through the door? That is within your control. One of your priorities should be adjusting the spiritual air in your home. Is it a place filled with the presence of God? Does the Holy Spirit dwell comfortably there? Does praise and worship flow from room to room? Is your home dedicated to God, to claim as His own, and have His way in every corner of it? Do people sense the presence of God and the peace that He brings into a home when it has been committed to Him?

Bless your house, pray in every room, and give each corner to the Lord. The difference will be amazing. Next, look at your surroundings and how things are arranged in every room. How you have your furniture arranged can affect your daily life. If it's cluttered, life can be chaotic. If it is orderly, life will be more peaceful. God is a God of order and highly concerned about where things are placed. Your home reveals your spiritual and mental condition. Are you confused or out of sorts? Is your house in order?

Do away with clutter and make way for space and air that allows you to breathe freely. This removes feelings of anxiety and makes room for peace. Order is important. It signals that things are settled and creates an air of stability. All these factors will be things that a man notes when he visits your home. Though he may not know exactly what he is looking for and why he feels what he feels, he will definitely have a reaction to you based on how he feels in your personal surroundings. Make him feel at home.

Texture

The garden had hangings of white and blue linen, fastened with cords of white linen and purple material to silver rings on marble pillars. There were couches of gold and silver on a mosaic pavement of porphyry, marble, mother-of-pearl and other costly stones (Esther 1:6).

*N*ot only was color utilized to display wealth and riches in the days of old, but a masterful blending of different textures was interwoven as well. It was a feast for the fingertips as well as the eyes and gave dimension to the room. Texture makes a man experience the room rather than just look at it. It welcomes him into your environment, embraces him, and holds him there. It pulls him into the moment with you.

There are different textures to your personality. You are not always soft, or hard, or smooth, or prickly. These textures make you interesting. They make a man want to touch and experience the different dimensions of you.

Texture in clothing is also important. Try textures that heighten his interest. Textures that make you attractive. Textures that fall in the right places, enhancing your figure and overall package. Soft and satiny, plush and warm. Wear textures that make him want to reach out and hold you, to experience and enfold you.

Artwork

*T*he absence or presence of artwork says a lot about you. How sentimental, creative, or aware of yourself are you? It will show in the things you surround yourself with. You will be attracted to pieces that mirror your heart, your desires, your fantasies. Artwork also adds a cultural touch to your home.

Just as paintings can take you beyond where you presently are when you look at them, artwork can draw your man and other visitors into your personal world.

Usually you will see a theme in people's homes. They tend to gravitate to the same types of paintings. This can be very revealing. On a visit to my parents' recently, I noticed all of their paintings were either of vast outdoor scenes or close-ups of flowers. Upon deeper investigation, I discovered that all the pictures of flowers had been chosen by my mother, while my father chose all of the outdoor scenery. I laughed when I commented that their choices were in keeping with their gender. Men see the big picture, while women tend to be drawn to the details.

Some are more eclectic in their tastes, choosing abstract paintings and sculptures, or mixing and matching unpredictable elements together. This reveals the mindset. Visitors always comment that my home looks like a museum. It truly reflects who I am and where I've been. As I've traveled, I've collected pieces to remind me of those places. Guests take delight in discovering these experiences through my eyes. Paintings of women and romantic scenes are everywhere. Most walk away knowing I am a romantic who enjoys being a woman.

What does your artwork tell a man about you? What would you like it to say? Choose your pieces accordingly. Don't just select things by number or because they are a good deal. Make sure they always express something about you. Throw in something a little unexpected for a pleasant surprise.

Though you might not think this is an area that men really take note of, don't let that be a deterrent to surrounding yourself with things that speak volumes about the woman within. It is the overall effect that he will take in. And in the process, he will learn a lot more about you.

Flowers and Plants

*N*ot having a green thumb is no excuse for not bringing life into a room. For many years, I avoided this. However, plants and flowers tell more than you know. Not only do they reveal you have an appreciation for God's creation, they speak of nurturing. Some plants need more care than others, so pick them according to your abilities but do *something*. Some gladiolas on your dining room table, or a rose in a bud vase on an end table, not only bring life and color into a room, they personify your femininity. The softer side of you. They serve as a quiet reminder to him that beauty is important to you. And perhaps when that man visits and sees the presence of flowers, he will be inspired to bring some on his next visit.

Photographs and Books

*H*ave you ever noticed how new visitors peruse your bookshelves and linger around the photographs you display? They are taking note of your interests and what's important to you. When they leave, they will know what you are curious about, what you care enough about to study.

Pictures divulge who is important in your life, whether that be family and friends or someplace where you collected pleasant memories. Photos say more than that. They will tell him if family is important to you. If relationships are something dear to you. They will even reveal if you are already covered by love in your world by the people you surround yourself with.

Your books will expose your depth. How much do you search for deeper truth or escape into fantasy? Are you learned or not a reader at all? A man of depth is looking for a complementary partner he can share and exchange ideas with. It is the silent things he takes note of that will tell him if you are up to the task.

Set Table

Since Emily Post faded off the scene, women have forgotten the value of setting an inviting table. The look of surprised delight on a man's face when looking at a nicely dressed table should remind you. Bring out the good stuff. Beautiful glasses, lovely silverware, wonderful plates. Serve him as if he is a distinguished guest. Visions of your care, effort, and concentrated preparation in honor of him will fill him with a feeling of being special. When you make him feel special, he will go out of his way to make you feel special too.

Lighting

Light is sweet, and it pleases the eyes to see the sun (Ecclesiastes 11:7).

*L*ight that is too bright will make you squint. Softer lighting will draw you in to see what is there. Set the lights in your home to complement you. Every movie star knows the importance of lighting. I know of many who will not enter a set until the lights are adjusted to hide every flaw and wrinkle. Light can cast harsh shadows or illuminate you softly. Single women, you should be cognizant of the effect of lighting in your home and make sure you are not sending mixed signals. Don't set a mood that makes it difficult to maintain your purity. Once married, you can continue to nurture romance by making the atmosphere in your home one that promotes intimacy. Light sets the mood for romance or distance. Whether it be candles or lamplight, illuminate the right subject in your home—you and the one you love.

Furniture

*I*n the Old Testament, God gave specific instructions on how to build things—even furniture. If God thought furniture was significant, there must be something to it. Your furniture will either make him want to stay or go. Make your home comfortable and inviting with furnishings that welcome and embrace him. Select furniture he can settle into. Use what you have. Spiff up old pieces with a fun finish and great throws. Make your house feel like home. A man is not comfortable in a house that does not give him permission to be himself.

Though decorating is important, your guests should never feel wary about where they place themselves. What they can or cannot touch. Where they can or cannot stand. Where they can or cannot sit. No, no. Every piece in your house should be something that someone can enjoy freely. Beautiful, but not so much of a showpiece that it causes discomfort. Less concentration on his surroundings leaves more room for him to concentrate on what is truly important—you.

Subtle Touches

*R*emember, it is the little things that make up the whole of your home and make you a welcome sight for his eyes.

Pillows

Make them cozy. Give him something to cuddle.

Rugs

Make his feet feel welcome. Give him a respite from the rough places he has traveled.

Coverings

Egyptian cottons. Beautiful sheets. Plush chenilles. Quilts. Throws on sofas. From Pier One to countless catalogs, make your selections creative to give pleasure to his eyes as well as his touch.

93 Color

*D*eep and moody. Soft and restful. Subtle and feminine. Rich and passionate. Nothing can affect your mood like color. It can invoke a bull to charge, make people lazy or productive, cause folks to linger or flee.

The newest trend in home decorating is color, color, and more color. Effects with color. Sponging, ragging, faux painting—you name it. A lot of energy and imagination goes into setting the mood in a room with color. Gone are stark white walls, or even safe creme. It's all about making things in the room pop. That includes you.

This is something that is not usually considered, but keep in mind the room you are in is your frame. Select colors that make you look beautiful in his eyes from every angle. What are you wearing?

For years, everything in my wardrobe was black. I traveled a lot, and that way everything was guaranteed to match. Simple, I thought, until one day one of my male friends said to me, "Why don't you ever wear any colors? I bet you would look incredible in red." One, I was shocked that he had noticed. And if he finally said it, how long had he been thinking about it? Second, the thought of that much vibrant color on my person scared me. However, I decided to try a red sweater. Well! You would have thought I had immersed myself in pheromones! Men were coming out of the woodwork! Needless to say, I've spiced up my wardrobe with touches of color ever since.

Go ahead and try it—color—in your clothing and in your home. Just a little dab will do ya!

Clothing

*D*on't just follow the latest fashion trend. Your clothes say way too much about you to allow others to rule your individuality. Pick your style and be faithful to it, updating it with subtle touches but never straying. Choose a classic foundation, a tasty color palette, and then add a touch of whimsy from time to time. A scarf here, a belt there. A little can go far and create interest.

Your clothing should not distract from who you are. It should accentuate the positives of your body and downplay the negative. It should complement you and play up your virtues, your coloring, and your figure.

After experimenting while shopping, I discovered what women think looks great is not necessarily what gets a man's attention. When trying on garments for my male friends and asking their opinion, it varied from what my girlfriends told me. My discussions with men about this uncovered a truly surprising fact: In most cases, what women think is sexy, men merely take as trying too hard.

"What do they like then?" you ask. They like clothes that are worn easily. Not too formal and "done to the nines." And definitely not too tight! They like you to be able to wear a pair of jeans as easily as you do a dress. They want a playmate as much as they do a showpiece. Be able to transition easily to one or the other.

Remember, clothing is the canvas where your womanly attributes are highlighted. Make sure the picture you present to him is one that will make him stop to admire and appreciate its beauty.

Accessories

*A*s with your home, the foundation is merely the beginning of presenting the entire picture. So pay attention to the little things you wear; they can make a big difference in the overall effect of how you present yourself.

Jewelry

Jewelry is the light you bring to yourself. Just as too much light can cause an undesirable glare, overdone jewelry can be a turnoff. Single women should be aware of the rings they wear lest they give the impression they are already taken. Precious metals and colored stones add beauty to any garment and set it off. They should be accents, not ornaments that complement your coloring. Remember, your jewelry should draw him in, not distract him from seeing the light shining in your eyes.

Shoes

Just as women have a thing about shoes, men do too. Names have been given to types of shoes I won't mention here, but you know what I'm talking about. Select shoes that give a feminine shape to feet and flatter the shape of your legs. Don't just look at your feet when selecting a shoe, check out the entire picture, because that is exactly what he is doing.

Scarves

Scarves are a wonderful way to add a touch of color and texture to your outfit that pulls his eyes toward you and gives him a hint of what you feel like. Isn't that the desired effect?

Caresses and Hugs

There is a time for everything, and a season for every activity under heaven...a time to embrace and a time to refrain (Ecclesiastes 3:1,5).

Just as John laid his head on the breast of Jesus, closeness allows you to hear each other's heartbeat. Knowing how to hold your husband will make him vulnerable to you. A caress and a hug are not just physical, they are a ministry. Hugs administer life and comfort. They draw him to you spiritually and emotionally. They allow you to connect with him in a personal way that excludes all others. Let your arms be a haven—a place where he wants to be. Be comfortable enough to reach past yourself and allow him into your personal space.

Warm, yielding, and inviting—everyone can use a good hug. Give them freely when it is appropriate.

Body

Be kind to your body. Care for it well. It is the only one you have. Nurture your outside as well as your inside. Touchable skin and a body a man enjoys holding are high on the list. Men are visual creatures. They respond to the external first. Be healthy, whole, and touchable. *Men have been in awe of a woman's body since the beginning of time.*

Take responsibility for making yours a body you will be proud to present to your mate on your wedding night as well as throughout your marriage.

Do the work it takes to maintain a sense of well-being. Eat right, sleep, and exercise. Do the things it takes to keep fit so that you have a body that is not only healthy and sound, but one that will not hinder you from being free to enjoy intimacy with your mate. If you feel good about your body, your mate will too.

98 Kiss

Let him kiss me with the kisses of his mouth—for your love is more delightful than wine (Song of Songs 1:2).

Kisses are more than kisses. They are an exchange of not only breath, but emotion. This is the place of giving yourself, where your inner woman is revealed. All the warmth, all the passion you possess is exposed with one kiss. Kisses are important to a man because they whisper promises to him of what your love will be like.

Keep it sweet. Make sure your breath is sweet and your lips are soft, subtle, and yielding. Make him feel welcome to know your heart. Singles, you must be honest with yourself. If a kiss causes you to struggle with self-control, you should refrain until you are within the safe confines of marriage. You must set your own personal boundaries to maintain your purity. But do it gently in order to keep your potential mate from feeling rejected. Explain that though you are very attracted to him, you feel a responsibility to help him keep your relationship pleasing to God. The reality is some of you are going to kiss anyway, so adopt this mindset—kisses are small appetizers, that's it. If he wants the main course, he has to sign up for the full-meal deal—a lifetime commitment.

Married women, never allow yourself to settle into a routine. Sweet kisses will serve as a refresher to any dry romance. Passionate kisses will keep the flame alive.

Heart

He who loves a pure heart and whose speech is gracious will have the king for his friend (Proverbs 22:11).

She has a good heart..." Funny how others can know that just from spending a short time in your presence. Out of the abundance of the heart the mouth speaks, and your heart will leave an indelible mark on the spirit of those you share yourself with. What draws a man to your heart? All the men I spoke with indicated it's the things that emanate from your heart. Faithfulness, purity, sincerity. A giving heart. Unselfish, unpretentious, and uncomplicated. Open, trusting without being naïve, unafraid of being transparent. This is the heart that touches a man and makes him want to reach out to you.

Free yourself from all bitterness and baggage from the past. Tear down the walls and trust your heart to God for safekeeping. Guard it only in the sense of being discerning of who you offer it to and then walk graciously with all you encounter. *The place you want to touch him most is in his heart, where his strength lies.* Adding your strength to his strength, taking nothing away. Adding to what is already there.

Want to win a man's heart? Then connect with him where it counts, heart to heart.

100 Mind

She [the queen of Sheba] came to Solomon and talked with him about all she had on her mind (2 Chronicles 9:1).

A man responds to a woman who is imaginative and thought-provoking. A woman who is not challenging mentally is like a toy he soon grows weary of. Touch the part of him that searches to be better with your thoughts and observations.

Avoid being double-minded. It causes trepidation in the heart of a man. Settle your heart and share solid beliefs and views. Set the course for growth in your relationship with empowering conversations, reassurances, and gentle thoughts that always keep you on his mind.

101 Attention

Ears that hear and eyes that see—the LORD has made them both (Proverbs 20:12).

Want to catch and keep the attention of a man? Then pay attention. Commit your focus to him when he is in your presence.

No one wants to speak and not be heard. So listen, really listen, and then follow through with actions that prove you really heard his heart. Just as God judges our hearts by our obedience, one of the aspects a man judges love by is how a woman pays attention to what he says and responds.

Single women, listen up: Make your man feel that he is the most brilliant, most fascinating man on the face of the earth. Most of all, make him feel secure in his pursuit of you by welcoming his company, tuning out all other distractions, and centering on him. When he feels important to you, he will strive to remain significant in your world.

Wives, pay attention: Give your man what he says he wants, not what you *think* he *needs*. There is a difference. Men want attention. Undivided, affectionate, wholehearted attention. In this respect, they are like little boys, constantly seeking reassurance that they are indeed loved and adored. Sound like too much work?

Keep in mind when you pay him attention, you will have his full attention as well.

Echoes of a man's mind...

Would you mind if I touched you?

I mean, really touched you...

I mean, touch you where it matters...

heart, spirit, and soul

your inner woman

the part of you that you hide

that is sacred?

Would you let me build an altar there,

where we can worship together

as one—

transparent and unashamed?

And would you mind if I looked at you?

I mean, really looked at you...

Past the you

that you've so carefully groomed

for me to see?

Past the tough exterior,

deep within your heart

where it's soft, warm, and vulnerable?

Would you let me fill you with reassurances

until I felt your defenses

yield in the palm of my hand

and respond to my invitation to love?

And then I'd like to hear you,

I mean, really hear you.

So...would you mind

if I eavesdropped on your thoughts,

if I overheard your daydreams

and made them all come true?

Then would you mind if I tasted you?

I mean, really taste you...

the bitterness of you...

the sweetness of you...

All the flavors of you

that make you so rare...

and unforgettable...

I'd like to savor your love

like a rich dessert...

And all that would be left

is the scent of you...

By the way, would you mind

if I breathed in your essence?

your life?

I promise I'd return it

   and treasure the memory

      of living through your senses.

   For then I would totally know you...

      and know how to love you in return...

Other Books by
Michelle McKinney Hammond

What to Do Until Love Finds You
Secrets of an Irresistible Woman
Where Are You, God?
The Power of Being a Woman
Get a Love Life
If Men Are Like Buses, Then How Do I Catch One?
Prayer Guide for the Brokenhearted
What Becomes of the Brokenhearted?
How to Be Blessed and Highly Favored
Get Over It and On With It
Wounded Hearts, Renewed Hope
Why Do I Say "Yes" When I Need To Say "No?"
Sassy, Single, & Satisfied
The Unspoken Rules of Love
In Search of the Proverbs 31 Man
101 Ways to Get and Keep His Attention
The DIVA Principle™
The DIVA Principle™—A Sistergirl's Guide

To correspond with Michelle McKinney Hammond,
you may write to her:
c/o Heartwing Ministries
P.O. Box 11052
Chicago, IL 60611
E-mail her at heartwingmin@yahoo.com
Or log on to her website at:
www.michellehammond.com or www.heartwing.org

For information on booking her for a
speaking engagement:
866-391-0955